AS History

UNIT 1

2ND EDITION

Edexcel

The Seeds of Evil: The Rise of National Socialism in Germany to 1933

Geoff Stewart

Series Editor: Derrick Murphy

Philip Allan Updates
Market Place
Deddington
Oxfordshire
OX15 0SE

Orders

Bookpoint Ltd, 130 Milton Park, Abingdon, Oxfordshire, OX14 4SB
tel: 01235 827720
fax: 01235 400454
e-mail: uk.orders@bookpoint.co.uk
Lines are open 9.00 a.m.–5.00 p.m., Monday to Saturday, with a 24-hour message
answering service. You can also order through the Philip Allan Updates website:
www.philipallan.co.uk

© Philip Allan Updates 2001
This edition © Philip Allan Updates 2006

ISBN-13: 978-1-84489-566-3
ISBN-10: 1-84489-566-1

This guide has been written specifically to support students preparing for
the Edexcel AS History Unit 1 examination. The content has been neither
approved nor endorsed by Edexcel and remains the sole responsibility of the
author.

Printed by MPG Books, Bodmin

Philip Allan Updates' policy is to use papers that are natural, renewable
and recyclable products and made from wood grown in sustainable forests.
The logging and manufacturing processes are expected to conform to the
environmental regulations of the country of origin.

Contents

Introduction

■ ■ ■

Content Guidance

■ ■ ■

Questions and Answers

Introduction

Aims of the unit

Unit 1 amounts to 20% of the whole A-level course or 40% of the AS award. It requires knowledge of the topic and the ability to assess and use the source material provided. The source-handling skills expected are similar to those required at GCSE but more developed. The difficulty of the source material and questions asked is less than for the full A-level set in Unit 6.

The total of marks for Unit 1 is 60. These are split roughly into 10 marks for knowledge of the topic and 50 marks for ability to handle the sources.

Handling the sources involves:
- interpreting, evaluating and using a range of source material
- explaining and evaluating interpretations of the historical events and topics studied

Knowledge involves:
- recalling, selecting and deploying historical knowledge accurately
- communicating knowledge and understanding of history in a clear and effective manner
- presenting historical explanations to show an understanding of appropriate concepts
- arriving at substantiated judgements

The emphasis of this unit is on the comprehension and manipulation of the source extracts rather than on a simple knowledge of the rise of the Nazis. As you will see in the Question and Answer section, question (a) is a test of skill in comprehension and assessment of the sources, and requires no information other than that provided in the extracts.

The other question, (b), carries the higher number of marks (40 out of 60). This question, as might be expected, is the more demanding as it requires both knowledge and the ability to manipulate the appropriate extracts. A good answer will keep a sharp focus on the question asked, combining both knowledge and the source materials provided.

It is extremely important to take note of the number of marks allocated to each section and to make sure that your effort is appropriate to the spread of marks. In other words, the response to question (b) should be roughly twice as long as the response to question (a).

When the word 'study' is used at the beginning of a question, it is an indication that no additional knowledge is required (although clearly such knowledge might help you to comprehend or evaluate the source). Where it is necessary to use your own knowledge, this will be stated clearly in the question.

The examination paper

On the examination paper for this unit you will be given sources. There will be either five or six of these, together adding up to roughly 500 words. One of the sources, usually the last, will be a secondary source. One of the sources may be visual or statistical. Before each source you will be given some information in italics. This is intended to help you understand the nature of the source and is particularly important when it comes to dealing with a visual source.

Three sample questions are given in the last section of this book. Study them carefully. In each case the sources are followed by a question in two parts.

- Part (a) requires comprehension and analysis of the sources and cross-referencing to reach a conclusion. Typically this will involve asking '**How far do the sources support the view that...?**' Where appropriate, the utility of one or all of the sources should be assessed in making the required judgement. This new-style part (a) is an amalgam of the old parts (a), (c) and (d). Like all of these, there is no need to bring in own knowledge. The question can and should be answered entirely from the sources provided.
- Part (b), as indicated on p. 4, is the more important, and requires knowledge and the use and analysis of two or three of the sources, which will have to be blended together in a focused fashion to produce an essay. A typical question will start with '**Do you agree with the view that...?**'

The layout of the questions on the examination paper is as follows:

(a) Study Sources 1, 2 and 3.
    How far do these three sources support the view that...?   (20 marks)
(b) Study Sources 4 and 5 and use your own knowledge.
    How important was...?   (40 marks)

How to use this guide

- Make sure you understand clearly the pattern of marks and the type of questions explained above.
- Although the emphasis of this unit is on the handling of sources rather than knowledge, there is still a body of facts that have to be known. Study carefully the outline material in the Content Guidance section. Try to master the vocabulary and the concepts given there. Sort out clearly in your mind the important individuals who figure in the events of the period in question. Remember the people in terms of the parties and groupings to which they belonged.
- The most important part of the guide is the Question and Answer section, which provides three examples of the sort of questions you will be asked. It is important to work through each of these, studying the two sample answers provided and the examiner's comments (preceded by the icon ✐). The first example is an A-grade response which, although not perfect, gives a good idea of what is required. The purpose of the second answer is to illustrate some of the common errors that students make.

The sources

There is a vast range of sources available to students studying the rise of the Nazi Party. New books appear almost daily on the subject. There are many collections of primary documents relevant to this topic and students should familiarise themselves with some of the different types of material available. The Question and Answer section of this guide contains an assortment of these. As with all sources of evidence used by historians, it is important to try to find out when and why a particular document was written. Usually the date will be given in italics before the extract, and some information will be provided to help you understand why this particular source was originally produced. Clearly it helps to know the political sympathies of the author. Was the author or illustrator a Nazi sympathiser or supporter? Was he or she an opponent of the Nazis. Bias is inevitable, but this does not mean that the sources are worthless to historians.

It is, of course, important to realise that people's opinions change over time and with circumstances. Hitler and the Nazi Party were no exception. Two of the most important sources of information used by historians in their study of the origins and development of the Nazi Party are:

- *Mein Kampf* ('My Struggle'), written by Hitler in 1924 and regularly used by historians to illustrate Hitler's opinions on a variety of subjects
- the so-called 25 *Points*, the Nazi Party programme written in 1920

Extracts from both these works are given in the Question and Answer section. How important these two documents are is open to debate. Some have argued that Hitler was later ashamed and embarrassed by much of what he had written in 1924. Doubt has also been cast on the value of the 25 *Points*, written as they were in the early days of the party. The Nazi Party of 1920 was very different from the mass party of 1933. The party was particularly adept at adjusting to circumstances, targeting the working class in the mid-1920s but switching effectively to win over the peasantry from 1928. In the early 1930s it was successful in gaining the support of large sections of the middle classes. Clearly its propaganda varied according to the circumstances. The examples given in the Question and Answer section are intended to illustrate both the flexibility and the considerable ambiguity that was present in the Nazi Party. In some ways the party was all things to all people because it lacked a clear-cut message. It was both socialist and nationalist, as its very name implies. Traditionally Hitler is considered a figure of the right, particularly by Marxists and those of left-wing persuasion. Yet to many contemporary conservatives he was a dangerous figure of the left, closely related to the communists he denounced. Many of the Nazis' most bitter opponents came from the ranks of the aristocracy and the traditional right.

'Who supported the Nazi Party, and why?' are two of the big questions within this topic that historians have tried to answer for decades. Many of the extracts used in the Question and Answer section are concerned with these two questions. The dates of such extracts must always be taken into account. This is particularly important when dealing with the rise of the Nazi Party, in view of its very rapid transformation between 1929 and 1933. Try to pay attention to the social class of the writer as this may be vital. However, just because one Hamburg schoolteacher supported (or opposed) the Nazi Party does not mean that all schoolteachers or all people in Hamburg were Nazi supporters or opponents. This also introduces the importance of geography. Nazi support varied from one part of Germany to another.

Don't forget that opponents can become supporters and supporters opponents. General Erich von Ludendorff worked closely with Hitler during the Munich Putsch but 10 years later, when Hitler became Chancellor, Ludendorff famously denounced him as 'accursed' and 'a man who would lead Germany into the abyss'.

The visual and statistical sources may pose particular problems to some candidates. With cartoons it is especially important to read and understand the accompanying information to enable you to make sense of them. A cartoon represents the opinion of one person — either that of the artist or the proprietor of the journal in which it appears — possibly both. It is likely, however, that it will also appeal to a wider audience, who will buy the journal in the expectation of certain opinions.

Statistical data have their own special pitfalls. Always look carefully to see what is being offered. Once again, dates are important. When election results are provided, make sure you understand what is referred to — number of MPs elected or percentage of the vote cast for a particular party. Look carefully at the relative performance of different parties. Finally, do not be intimidated by the appearance of statistical data. Some people are frightened by statistics, but they are a very useful way of presenting a complex mass of information simply.

Examinable skills

The ability to comprehend a source is perhaps the most basic one required in this unit. To achieve this there is no substitute for simple practice. Analysis, evaluation and interpretation follow on from the basic capacity for comprehension.

In answering the first question, it is important not to simply write out the sources in the hope that this will provide the examiner with the answer. It is essential to select the appropriate material to answer the question set. The answer should be as brief and concise as possible.

The question requires you to offer explanations based on the three extracts. Your answer should have a clear direction and the question should not simply be left to the final sentence before you openly address it. Where necessary you should try to develop the skill to make the appropriate inference and deduction from the extracts. Try always to make a clear opening statement that indicates the direction in which your answer is going. Try to develop your points in a logical and structured way with appropriate quotations and support from the extracts. These should never be too lengthy. You should be using the extracts, not allowing yourself to be dictated to by them. Cross-referencing is the key skill, but some element of evaluation of source utility may be necessary and desirable. The source attribution is vital in this and should be considered carefully along with the content of the source itself.

The part (b) question probably demands the most skills. Focus on the question asked is essential and it is vital that both appropriate evidence from the sources and own knowledge is integrated into a sustained analysis. It is worth emphasising here that one of the skills that examiners look for is the ability to **communicate clear, concise and logical arguments substantiated by relevant evidence**. The ability to write clearly and attractively is one of the most valuable in the historian's armoury. It is a skill to be worked on constantly. There is no quick fix to achieve literary polish — but candidates can remember that, as in all essays, there should be a clear introductory statement and, most important of all, a conclusion to draw together the argument advanced throughout the answer.

Content
Guidance

The areas covered by Unit 1 are:
- the Nazi Party from its formation to the Beer Hall Putsch
- Nazi beliefs about, and policies towards, Weimar politics and society
- economic, social and political reasons for the support of, and opposition to, the Nazis to 1933
- Hitler and German politics, 1929–33

The main focus is on the growth and development of the Nazi Party between 1920 and March 1933. A knowledge and understanding of Weimar politics is essential to this. You will need to understand why Hitler and the Nazis so detested the young republic. Though no questions on foreign policy will be set, a knowledge of the Treaty of Versailles and an understanding of the hostility it evoked are vital to understanding the success of the Nazis.

To help you appreciate what you will need to learn, the subject matter of Unit 1 has been broken down in the Content Guidance section in two ways. First, there is an outline of topics — for use as a checklist for revision before the exam. Second, there is an introduction to the basic information, concepts and personalities you will need to know about. These are covered in five areas:

(1) Germany and Hitler to 1920 (pp. 12–17)
(2) The social, economic and political background to the rise of the Nazis (pp. 18–22)
(3) The quiet years, 1925–28 (pp. 22–26)
(4) The Nazi breakthrough to power, 1929–33 (pp. 26–33)
(5) The consolidation of power, January–March 1933 (pp. 33–36)

Each of these is followed by listings of concepts and key figures. Words which appear in these listings are emboldened in the text.

Outline of topics

Background to 1920
Germany in 1914 — the Second Reich
The experience of the First World War, 1914–18
The revolution of 1918
The Treaty of Versailles, 1919
The Weimar Constitution
Weimar political parties and politics

The economic, social and political context, 1920–33
The crisis years, 1920–23
The golden years, 1924–28
The economic crisis, 1929 — agriculture, industry and trade
The onset of the political crisis, 1929–30
The political crisis, 1930–33

Hitler and the early years of the Nazi Party to 1924
Hitler 1889–1920
Hitler's ideas and the formation and growth of the Nazi Party in Munich,
   1920–22
The Munich Beer Hall Putsch, 1923
Landsberg and *Mein Kampf*, 1924

The re-establishment of the party and its organisation, 1925–28
Hitler reasserts control — Bamberg
The social profile of party membership — who was a Nazi and why
Party structure and planning
The 1928 election and the situation in rural areas

The breakthrough to national importance, 1928–30
The appeal of the National Socialist German Workers' Party (NSDAP)
   to the peasants
The appeal to youth
Hitler, Hugenberg and the Young Plan
Goebbels and the election of 1930

The struggle for power, September 1930–January 1933
The role of the SA — Stennes' Revolt
The drift of the middle classes to the NSDAP — the communist menace
Hitler's balancing act — the Harzburg Front and relations with the
   German National People's Party (DNVP)

Germany and Hitler to 1920

Germany 1914–20

Germany in 1914 was the greatest power in mainland Europe. It had the world's most powerful army and the world's second most powerful navy. In every way Germany appeared to be one of the world's leading nations. German industry was second only to that of the USA in volume of production. Since the beginning of the 1900s Germany had overtaken Britain as an industrial power. It was in the new industries of the twentieth century that Germany particularly shone. In chemicals, engineering and the new electrical industries Britain was left far behind. As the German economy expanded, wages and living standards rose. In the 1880s Germany developed a national welfare system in advance of any other country, with old age pensions and health insurance. But Germans did not live by bread alone. In the realm of ideas and culture Germany was pre-eminent. The greatest names in philosophy and music were German. Not surprisingly most Germans, whatever their political persuasion, felt rightly proud of the achievements of their new nation. None felt this more than their ruler, **Kaiser Wilhelm II**.

This new Germany was created in 1871, when the German state of Prussia conquered France and joined with the other German states in a new German empire — the **Second Reich**. The King of Prussia had become the German Emperor, head of an imperial federation of smaller German states like Baden and Bavaria. This new Germany was no democracy — despite the existence of a parliament (the Reichstag). The Kaiser appointed the chancellor (prime minister) and the Kaiser was the only person who could remove him. The Kaiser was also head of the army, which enjoyed enormous prestige. A landowning gentry and aristocracy dominated the army and political life. The new industrial élite shared power with them, but very much as junior partners.

The largest party in the Reichstag in 1914 was the Social Democratic Party of Germany (SPD), which claimed to speak for the new and growing working class. There was considerable tension between the socialists, who wanted to abolish the monarchy and turn Germany into a real democracy, and the old élite who, not surprisingly, felt somewhat threatened by this large party that spoke the language of revolution and **Marxism.** In reality the SPD was no longer a revolutionary party — but it wanted real political changes and it frightened the Kaiser and the army.

The outbreak of war in 1914 seemed at first to help solve some of these internal problems. Even the SPD rallied to the war effort, believing that the war was a just one forced on Germany by an envious coalition of France, Russia and Britain. This spirit of unity and national pride was something the Nazis were to seek to recapture after the war. As the war continued — with mounting casualties at the front and growing hunger and suffering at home — so this spirit of unity began to unravel. The British naval blockade of Germany, by cutting off food supplies, caused immense suffering. It has been estimated that half a million Germans died of malnutrition. By 1917, with the war in its third year and stalemate on the Western Front with France, the cries for peace increased, as did the number of strikes in Germany. The collapse of Russia in 1917 offered one last hope of victory despite the USA's declaration of war in April 1917. However, if Germany failed to act quickly it would be overwhelmed by the USA's economic might.

By late 1917, critical decisions were being made by the army. Germany had turned into a virtual military dictatorship under **Field Marshal Paul von Hindenburg** and his deputy, **General Erich von Ludendorff**. Hindenburg and Ludendorff decided to gamble everything on one last great push for victory in March 1918. It nearly succeeded. The German armies came closer to Paris than at any time since 1914. It cost 800,000 casualties, however — losses the Germans could not afford. A devastating Allied counterattack followed, beginning in July.

Germany's failure to achieve victory saw morale in the army plummet. At home, strikes multiplied. The war was lost and even the army High Command recognised this — although later they were to deny it. Ludendorff recommended that the Kaiser appoint a new liberal government to seek peace.

Many Germans still believed that a generous peace would be offered by the Allies — in line with the '14 Points' laid down by US President Wilson in January 1918. But this expectation was unreal. Germany was in a far weaker position by October. Great suffering had been inflicted on France and Allied troops in the meantime. Germany had imposed a brutally harsh treaty on Russia in March 1918. The Allies offered an armistice (ceasefire), to take effect on 11 November 1918. Details of a permanent peace would be given later. The Germans agreed, signing up to the armistice in a railway carriage in a clearing in the forest of Compiègne.

The events of the autumn of 1918 were later to be shrouded in myth and lies. Many Germans convinced themselves that they had been tricked by the Allies: that they could have fought on and would certainly have done so had they known of the harshness of the treaty that was to be offered them in 1919. There was a widespread belief, held by many in the army, that Germany had been stabbed in the back by revolutionaries and strikers. Jews were said to have played a major part in this, a view held by Hitler and, incidentally, by the Kaiser himself. It was convenient for many — not least those in the military who had lost their nerve in 1918 — to blame defeat on a nebulous conspiracy of 'reds', foreigners and politicians — those later described by Hitler as the **November Criminals**.

Revolution accompanied the armistice in Germany. The Kaiser fled to Holland and a republic was proclaimed. In the minds of many, the republic was associated with national humiliation and the end of the monarchy. This humiliation became more pronounced when the terms of the peace treaty were made clear to the Germans in 1919. The loss of Alsace and Lorraine to France could be accepted; the loss of so much territory to Poland could not. Over 1 million Germans found themselves citizens of the new Polish state. The Allies had claimed that the treaty was based on the principle of self-determination, yet millions of Austrian Germans were forbidden to join the Reich. Germany's colonies were taken away and distributed among the victorious Allies. Most Germans convinced themselves that the whole treaty was grossly unfair.

The enforced disarmament of Germany was bitterly resented. Its magnificent army was reduced to 100,000 men, smaller than the army of the new and despised state of Poland. Its new navy was destroyed and Germany was forbidden to build a replacement. Germany was to have no air force and the army was to have no tanks. The left bank of the Rhine was to be permanently demilitarised and Allied troops were to maintain garrisons on the right bank for 15 years. Most resented of all was the so-called 'war guilt' clause. Germany was declared to be responsible for the First World War — and faced a huge bill for its cost, imposed by the Allies. These reparations, more than anything else, were to make the *diktat* of the Treaty of Versailles a source of anger for many Germans.

In January 1919 a group of extremist socialists tried to seize power in a confusing revolution. It was crushed by the *Freikorps* and the moderate socialist government of **Friedrich Ebert**. A similar 'red' rising took place in Munich in the spring and was crushed by the army. Meanwhile, a battered and starving Germany was given a new constitution. To avoid the revolution in Berlin, delegates met in the nearby town of Weimar — hence the new regime was called the Weimar Republic. It was carefully constructed to try to provide Germany with its first real taste of democracy. The head of state, the president, was to be elected every 7 years. The president appointed the chancellor, who would head the government of the Reich. It was assumed that the chancellor would enjoy the support of the majority of the political parties in the German parliament, or Reichstag. There were to be elections every 4 years using a simple system of proportional representation. Electors voted for a party and each party produced a list of candidates numbered in order of importance within the party. The result of this system was that each party won a proportion of parliamentary seats directly related to its share of the votes cast. However, the system tended to prevent any one party having an effective majority. It encouraged the formation of a large number of **political parties** representing many different shades of political opinion — **monarchists**, conservatives, liberals and socialists. It ensured that every government was a coalition. During the Weimar years strong and effective decision-making was difficult and governments came and went with regularity.

Hitler and the forerunners of the NSDAP

In many ways Hitler was a very ordinary man made extraordinary by circumstance. He was born in 1889 into a lower-middle-class family on the Austrian side of the German–Austrian border. From his home town he made his way to Vienna in 1907. This was then a German city, but as the capital of a vast and largely Slav empire it contained many races, including a large Jewish minority. **Anti-Semitism** was rife and was already part of the currency of city politics. The then Mayor of Vienna, Carl Lüger, was a noted anti-Semite.

Hitler was heavily influenced by the ideas and emotions in the operas of **Richard Wagner**, spending much of his small private allowance on tickets for these grand events. He loved the magical world, where good and evil wrestled in an eternal struggle. He also absorbed the rabid German nationalism preached by street-corner orators and present in many cheap pamphlets. He increasingly saw life as a struggle between Jewish demons and German superheroes. Hitler absorbed the twin bedrock ideas of his life — racialism and nationalism — before the First World War. However, it was the events of 1918–19 that translated his prejudices into passions. Hitler blamed Germany's defeat in 1918 on the Jews. He returned to Munich in 1919, only to have his growing anti-Semitism confirmed by the prominent role Jews played in the abortive revolution there. Hitler increasingly believed that there existed a vast, all-embracing Jewish conspiracy to destroy civilisation. Were not Jews dominant among the Bolsheviks in Russia? Had not Jewish capital in the USA, Britain and France mobilised those countries for the defeat of Germany? Passion and hatred gave power to his voice. Simple, easily understood prejudices poured out to the first political audiences to hear him in Munich in 1920. The simplicity of his message ensured a favourable reception in a city looking for scapegoats — tired and exhausted by war and revolution.

In some ways what Hitler was offering was a new political religion shaped for the age of the common individual. Even before the First World War all those devices that would have kept Hitler firmly in check were weakening. The German philosopher Nietzsche had famously declared God to be dead. Traditional religion and churches were losing their grip. The old ruling élites were being challenged. An age of mass consumption and mass ideas was being born. Kings and emperors were replaced by politicians telling the people what they wanted to hear in language they could readily grasp. The First World War speeded the destruction of the old world, particularly in Germany. With the Kaiser gone, a new icon was needed. The returning disillusioned troops were particularly vulnerable to the sort of simplistic message that Hitler propounded. The war had brutalised many and made violence respectable. The new National Socialist German Workers' Party (NSDAP), founded in 1920, was to provide a home for soldiers like Ernst Röhm, who flaunted his contempt for conventional morality. The displaced Baltic German Alfred Rosenberg, fleeing from the Bolsheviks, also joined the new party, echoing Hitler's bitter anti-Jewish sentiments and racial analysis of the world.

Glossary and concepts

anti-Semitism — hostility towards Jews. There was widespread anti-Jewish feeling in France and Russia in the 1890s. From Russia came one of the most famous pieces of anti-Jewish propaganda, the Protocols of the Elders of Zion. This claimed to show a worldwide Jewish conspiracy and it certainly influenced many Nazi writers and thinkers.

diktat — word used to describe the Treaty of Versailles, meaning 'dictate'. The German delegates at the peace conference were not given the option to negotiate but were presented with a document that they had to sign, or else face renewal of the war.

Freikorps — paramilitary organisations established after the end of the First World War. Members were often drawn from ex-officers of the German army. They were active on the eastern border of Germany, defending Germans in the chaos which followed the border changes of the Versailles Treaty. They also played a major part in attacking left-wing revolutionaries in German cities.

Marxism — a set of political beliefs based on the works of Karl Marx. Marx claimed to have invented scientific socialism, showing the inevitable triumph of the working class or proletariat over the bourgeoisie. The Social Democratic Party of Germany (SPD) claimed to be Marxist but by 1914 had lost much of its revolutionary fervour. The Bolshevik revolution in Russia brought revolutionary Marxists to power there and they claimed that they would spread Marxism throughout Europe. Marxists believed in the common ownership of the means of production, distribution and exchange, i.e. they wanted the state to take over most forms of property. This created fear among those with property.

monarchists — people in Weimar Germany who supported the return of the monarchy and the abolition of the republic. The DNVP was a monarchist party opposed to the revolution of 1918.

November Criminals — those blamed by Hitler for the loss of the war and for the Treaty of Versailles. These included many of the leading politicians of the Weimar Republic.

political parties — Weimar Germany had a number of significant political parties. The DNVP (German National People's Party) was a conservative party drawing its support from rich landowners and big business. It was opposed to the Weimar Republic and was anxious to see the return of the monarchy. The DVP (German People's Party) was a moderate conservative party drawing support from the middle classes and business community. It was prepared to work with other parties to produce coalition democratic government. Its leading member was Gustav Stresemann, who became Chancellor in 1923 and then served as Foreign Minister until his death in 1929. The DDP (Germany Democratic Party) was a liberal party which supported the Weimar Republic. It enjoyed support from the lower middle classes and small farmers. The Centre Party was a religious or confessional party which spoke for Catholics and the Catholic Church. It drew support from south and western Germany. Unlike the other parties, it crossed class boundaries in its support. The SPD was the largest party of the Weimar Republic and its most consistent supporter. It was nominally Marxist but in reality it was a moderate reformist party, drawing its support from the skilled working class in the urban areas of Germany. The KPD, the Communist Party of Germany, was thoroughly Marxist and closely connected to the new Bolshevik government in Moscow (from which it received support). It normally gained around 10% of the vote, usually from the younger workers in the big cities like Hamburg and Berlin.

Second Reich — alternative name for the German Empire between 1871 and 1918. The First Reich had ended in 1806 and had dated back to its founder, Charlemagne.

Key figures

Friedrich Ebert (1871–1925) — a moderate socialist and a leader of the SPD who became the first president of the Weimar Republic. His cooperation with the army in 1919 was vital in crushing the extreme left wing and preventing a Russian-style revolution.

Field Marshal Paul von Hindenburg (1847–1934) — professional soldier drawn from an aristocratic east German background who became a national hero in 1914 when he defeated two Russian armies. He became Commander-in-Chief in 1916 and remained the nominal head of Germany's fighting forces until 1918. In 1925 he was persuaded by the political parties of the right to stand as President. He won and brought stability to the Weimar Republic. He remained President until his death in 1934.

General Erich von Ludendorff (1865–1937) — professional German soldier and usually held to be the brains behind the partnership he shared with Hindenburg during the First World War. After the war he became associated with various right-wing causes and drifted into alliance with Hitler in 1923. He escaped prosecution for the Munich Putsch and became increasingly suspicious of Hitler, whom he criticised.

Richard Wagner (1813–83) — German composer who had enormous influence upon Hitler. The romantic operas known as the Ring Cycle, composed between 1853 and 1874, particularly moved the young Hitler, who was later to claim that a knowledge of Wagner was essential to understand National Socialism.

Kaiser Wilhelm II (1859–1941) — third and last emperor of modern Germany. He abdicated in November 1918 and spent the rest of his life in Holland as an exile. Like Hitler, he blamed the Jews for the Germans having lost the First World War.

The social, economic and political background to the rise of the Nazis

The Weimar Republic

The first 4 years of the Weimar Republic, between 1919 and 1923, might easily have been the last. The republic was beset by problems, so much so that a foreign observer could have been forgiven for thinking the whole democratic experiment a disaster. A lot of Germans certainly did. These years witnessed the slide into **hyperinflation**. Many middle-class Germans were ruined. Those living on fixed pensions or relying on cash savings saw their value dwindle to nothing. Those who had patriotically bought government bonds during the war now found them worthless. In January 1920 the exchange rate had fallen to 65 marks to US$1. By 15 November 1923, US$1 was worth 42,000,000,000,000 marks.

Germany's effective bankruptcy brought one benefit for the government — though at a terrible price for the German people. The falling value of the mark eroded the vast and unsustainable mountain of debt that the First World War had bequeathed to the nation. However, economic chaos left the middle class disillusioned from the first with the new democratic Germany, distancing the republic from a natural constituency of support. The introduction of a new currency on 15 November 1923 was eventually to bring stability, but it did not restore prosperity to those who had been ruined.

Politically, the years 1919–23 were marked by many of the signs of a society in disintegration. Political assassination became commonplace, the victims being for the most part supporters of democracy and the perpetrators being drawn from the radical right who hated the new republic. Most army officers disliked the democratic republic and clung to the traditions of the empire. Judges, senior civil servants and university professors longed, for the most part, for the return of the monarchy. The judges showed their bias in the way they treated the perpetrators of political assassination. Murders of figures on the right were more likely to carry the death penalty than murders of figures on the left.

The new republic was threatened with revolt from both left and right. In 1920 a group of ex-army officers under General von Luttwitz and a senior civil servant, Dr Kapp, tried to seize power by force. They were defeated by a general strike. In the same week as these events were taking place in Berlin, a communist group of workers tried to seize power in the Ruhr, the industrial heartland of Germany. This uprising was crushed by the army. A year later there were fresh communist disturbances in Hamburg and central Germany. Many property owners were terrified that Germany would go the same way as Russia, where the new Bolshevik government was consolidating its power.

Bedevilling the government was the need to meet Allied demands for reparations. This added to the weakness of the currency. The nation's gold and foreign currency reserves were exhausted. In desperation, Germany resorted to trying to pay in kind with, for example, telegraph poles and coal, but the British already had too much of the latter and the French demand for the former was strictly limited. In 1922 Germany declared that it could no longer pay.

The French retaliated by occupying the Ruhr. German workers went on strike in protest and were supported by the Weimar government, which met the bill by printing money. Germany's currency went into free fall throughout 1923. Foreign visitors could live like kings on their dollars and pounds, much to the resentment of native Germans. Unsurprisingly, 1923 brought fresh outbreaks of violence from both right and left. In the autumn there were communist risings in Saxony that later spread to Hamburg and Thuringia. In Munich, Hitler felt his time had come. His abortive attempt at a coup — the Munich Beer Hall **Putsch** — was launched in November. The Reichstag elections showed gains for the Communist Party and the extreme right. Democracy seemed — and was — far from secure.

The NSDAP from 1920 to December 1924

In January 1919 Anton Drexler, a locksmith, founded a small and insignificant political party called the German Workers' Party, or DAP. It met in a pub and the party funds were kept in a cigar box. Drexler and his few comrades seemed to feel that the parties of the left lacked patriotism and that the parties of the right lacked social conscience. His party, he hoped, would combine the two.

Hitler returned to Munich in 1919 and witnessed the traumatic events of the attempt to seize power by German Bolsheviks. He remained with the army, serving as a political intelligence officer. The army was intent on keeping an eye on potential troublemakers. Drexler's party was seen as a potential source of trouble and Hitler was sent to observe their meetings. He appears to have been so impressed by the party's ideas that he joined in September. He continued in the army until March 1920.

The party he joined was one of many similar ***völkisch*** groups that existed in Germany. There were 15 alone in Munich, symptomatic of the discontent of postwar Germany. All shared a hatred of the Treaty of Versailles and a sense of betrayal by the politicians of the republic. Most were bitterly anti-Semitic. While still officially a member of the army, Hitler, with Drexler, drew up the DAP's political programme, known as the *25 Points*. It was to remain unaltered although largely ignored.

Hitler was a considerable catch for the small party. He quickly showed a talent for public speaking far beyond that of any other member. He became its biggest attraction, capable of bringing crowds to meetings and thus covering the party's expenses. DAP membership grew. In January 1920 there had been only 190 party members. By the end of the year this had grown to 2,000. In December 1920 the party was able to fund its own newspaper, the *Völkischer Beobachter*.

For Hitler's political career, 1921 was to prove a vital year. A major dispute developed within the ranks of the newly renamed National Socialist German Workers' Party (NSDAP or Nazi Party). Some members wanted to merge with another rival right-wing fringe party. Hitler objected. Compromise and negotiation were not his way. It was all or nothing. When he appeared to be losing the argument, he resigned from the party. It was a tremendous gamble but it paid off. The fledgling NSDAP could not afford to lose its best speaker. Hitler was welcomed back in triumph in July, made leader and granted dictatorial powers within the party. Increasingly he referred to himself as the drummer, the man who would mobilise the masses for Germany's regeneration. He still does not appear to have thought of himself as the would-be dictator of Germany — merely as the person who would make Germany's regeneration possible.

The other major development of 1921 was the formation of the *Sturmabteilung* (SA) (literally the 'Storm Section' but often referred to as the brownshirts). The SA's origins went back to 1920 when the party needed bouncers to protect its political meetings. A group was formed to provide this service — becoming known as the gym and sports section of the party. In July 1921 this section was renamed the SA. The key figure in the SA's development was **Ernst Röhm**, a brutal former frontline captain who enjoyed violence. He filled the SA with similar-minded ex-soldiers who liked nothing better than a punch-up with rival political groups. The knuckle-duster and the cosh were important ingredients in the early days of the rise of the Nazis. Another significant figure in the early SA was Lieutenant Klintsch. Klintsch was suspected of being involved in the assassination of the Reich Foreign Minister in 1922. Within the SA he spent much of his time ensuring that the same did not happen to Hitler, whose bodyguard he became.

By the beginning of 1922 NSDAP membership reached 6,000 but it was still largely confined to Munich. However, during 1922 the party expanded into the north of Bavaria, achieving a real base in the Protestant part of the state, especially around the ancient city of Nuremberg. The secret of this success lay in the willingness of the NSDAP to clash violently with their political opponents. This they did in a major demonstration in the town of Coburg, fighting a pitched battle with supporters of the SPD. Also in 1922, the NSDAP enjoyed an enormous stroke of luck when the leader of a rival right-wing group in Nuremberg, Julius Streicher, offered his and his party's allegiance to Hitler. The following year Streicher established another Nazi newspaper, *Der Stürmer*, which offered a diet of popular anti-Semitism heavily spiced with sex and violence.

The year 1922 offered Hitler and the Nazis another influential model of political action. In Italy, Mussolini had come to power as Prime Minister after what was, effectively, a political coup known as 'the march on Rome'. For propaganda purposes this was portrayed as a seizure of power and became part of fascist legend. In reality it had more in common with a publicity stunt — but Mussolini was not one to allow truth to get in the way of his own political progress. In November 1922 one of Hitler's sidekicks in the party proclaimed in Munich, 'Germany's Mussolini is called Adolf Hitler'. The idea of seizing power through direct action clearly had an appeal within the NSDAP.

By 1923 the party had a membership of 20,000. In the course of this year of hyperinflation and domestic crises, membership was to touch 55,000. The French occupation of the Ruhr in January 1923 triggered what seemed to be a terminal crisis for the Weimar Republic. Nationalist outrage reached a frenzied peak. An anti-republican government came to power in Bavaria. Hitler — in cooperation with the First World War Commander Ludendorff — became convinced that he and others on the right in Bavaria could lead a march on Berlin to overthrow the republican democracy there. He assumed the cooperation of the Bavarian authorities and the German army stationed in Bavaria. This was the origin of the famous Munich Beer Hall Putsch in November. Hitler badly overestimated the broader political and public support available for such a move. He failed to win over the conservative political leaders of the state of Bavaria. The following day, in desperation, he launched a street march that ended in disaster. Armed police opened fire on the marching ranks of the NSDAP. Hitler's supporter, **Hermann Goering**, received a bullet in the groin and the man marching next to Hitler was shot dead. Hitler was arrested for treason and could reasonably expect the death penalty. The NSDAP was banned.

Hitler's trial, however, turned into a political triumph. The wide coverage it received in the press made him, for the first time, a national figure in Germany. He was the hero of the fanatic right — the man who had stood up for Germany in a time of need. The judge was sympathetic and Hitler received a sentence of 5 years' detention in the fortress-prison of Landsberg. While in prison, Hitler was treated as a celebrity. The terms of his imprisonment were not harsh. He had the best room available. He could see visitors and mix with other party members who were also in jail. And he had the time to write *Mein Kampf* ('My Struggle'), his very own political testament. After having served only a fraction of his sentence Hitler was released, just before Christmas 1924.

Glossary and concepts

hyperinflation — crisis involving the value of the currency when prices increase so rapidly that money loses almost all value. Good for debtors, bad for savers.

Mein Kampf ('My Struggle') — Hitler's autobiography and reflections on life, as well as a type of political manifesto. *Mein Kampf* was published in two volumes in 1925 and 1926.

putsch — an attempt to seize power by force.

völkisch — racial or ethnic.

Key figures

Hermann Goering (1893–1945) — joined the Nazi Party in 1922, and was a good catch for the party. His father had been governor of German southwest Africa and he himself was an officer in the German Air Force in the First World War, achieving fame as an air ace. He was badly injured in the Munich Putsch but became a Nazi MP in 1928. He was one of only two Nazis to be included in Hitler's first Cabinet in 1933. Throughout most of the 1930s he was second in importance only to Hitler in the party. On the establishment of the Third Reich he became Prime Minister of Prussia and Reich Air Minister — in charge of the *Luftwaffe*, the new German Air Force. Goering became Hitler's deputy in 1938 but lost influence during the course of the Second World War. He was tried in Nuremberg in 1945 but committed suicide before he could be executed.

Ernst Röhm (1887–1934) — served as a captain in the First World War and joined the Nazi Party shortly after Hitler. He enjoyed the excitement of violence and developed the SA in its early days. When the Munich Putsch failed he went abroad, but he was reappointed as commander of the SA in 1930, a post he held until June 1934, when he died in the Night of the Long Knives.

The quiet years, 1925–28

Political, social and economic background

Having survived the first 4 years of the 1920s it began to look, by 1925, as if the Weimar Republic might take root and provide Germany with both stable government and prosperity. A new currency was introduced at the end of 1923. In the course of 1924 the French were persuaded to withdraw from the Ruhr and a new deal was struck on reparations. Germany's relations with both France and Britain improved under the skilful guidance of **Gustav Stresemann**. In 1926 Germany entered the League of Nations. Once more Germany commanded a place as one of the great powers of Europe. More importantly, the German economy began to flourish. Exports boomed and new technology helped to produce new jobs. Investment flooded into the country from the USA. American banks lent money to the German government, to local authorities and to German companies. American companies set up in Germany and something of the prosperity of the USA in the 1920s came to the country.

The economic prosperity was in some ways matched and mirrored by political stability. In 1925 the socialist President, Friedrich Ebert, died and was replaced by the conservative Field Marshal Paul von Hindenburg. Hindenburg proved something of a substitute monarch, reassuring the middle classes and gaining the loyalty of the army who, if they did not love the republic, would at least accept it with Hindenburg at its head. The Reichstag elections of December 1924 and 1928 showed a decline in support for the more extreme parties. The NSDAP had picked up 6.6% of the vote in May 1924; this fell to 3% in December and was down to 2.6% in 1928. The Communist Party's share of the vote fell from 12.6% to 9% in December 1924, recovering slightly in 1928 to 10.6%. In 1928 the longest-serving coalition government of Germany was formed under Hermann Müller of the SPD. It was to last until March 1930. The political assassinations that marked and marred the early years of the Weimar Republic declined sharply. It appeared that Germany had achieved stability. Yet Foreign Minister Stresemann believed the republic was 'dancing on a volcano' — and a close analysis of the situation could produce worrying conclusions.

The prosperity of the new industries was not matched by that of traditional heavy industry. Agriculture remained the biggest single employer in Germany (with over 30% of the workforce) and was in serious trouble as prices of agricultural products tumbled. Many employers increasingly resented the concessions granted to workers in the early days of the Weimar Republic. They thought the power of trade unions had grown too much and sought to claw back what they felt they had lost in 1919 and 1920. Even the prosperity of new industries was fragile, resting upon foreign export markets and constant new supplies of capital from the USA. If the capital should dry up or the export markets become saturated, then disaster could ensue.

Although the Weimar Republic had fewer political problems between 1925 and 1928, there was still cause for concern. Governments came and went with surprising rapidity, even if some ministerial posts remained in experienced hands (the position of foreign secretary was occupied by Stresemann for 5 years). There was a failure to take tough decisions. Taxation was unpopular and government spending popular. Balancing these two political truths is one of the eternal conundrums of government. Weimar Germany had first tried to solve it by printing money — with disastrous consequences in 1923. By 1925 this was no longer an option. The solution was to borrow. The federal government in Berlin, and state and even city authorities, borrowed heavily to provide a range of popular services and benefits. The policy worked well while capital was readily available. However, much of the borrowing was irresponsible.

Authorities took out short-term loans to pay for long-term projects, repaying debts as they fell due with fresh loans. Political parties still remained largely class-based or — in the case of the Centre Party — rooted in one religious community. The system of proportional representation, with its use of the list system, gave power to the party bosses in Berlin and the regional capitals. They determined the order of the candidates on the list. The link with local communities was fragile and voters became disillusioned with party politics. An ageing group of party political supremos made deals behind closed doors. The system could be tolerated as long as there was prosperity but would find it hard to deal with a real crisis.

Hitler and the NSDAP: consolidation and survival

On Hitler's release from Landsberg prison at the end of 1924, his priority was to get the ban lifted on his party. This he rapidly succeeded in doing after backstairs negotiations with senior politicians in Bavaria. He began to show real political skill, distancing himself from General Ludendorff, who was increasingly unpopular in Catholic Bavaria. He promised that the Nazi Party would not attempt any further putsch but would seek power through the ballot box.

By 1925 Hitler had reached two important conclusions with enormous consequences. First, he resolved never again to challenge the armed forces of the state but to play the Weimar Republic at its own democratic game. Second, he began to think of himself not merely as the drummer, gaining support for some other saviour of the nation, but as the chosen one, the man selected by providence to rescue Germany from humiliation and division.

Although the ban on the NSDAP was lifted, a ban was imposed on Hitler's speaking in public in most German states. He was allowed a platform only at private party meetings. The politicians of Weimar Germany calculated that this deprived the NSDAP of its chief weapon. Perhaps they were right. However, Hitler had other tasks he needed to turn to. He had to reassert his personal control over the Nazi movement and he had to pay some attention to party organisation, particularly outside Bavaria.

The Nazi Party was riddled with divisions, personal and political. Hitler saw it as his priority to re-found the party, based on absolute obedience to his position as leader. The finer points of policy could be ignored. There was to be no debate on the *25 Points*. The question was not to be raised of how socialist the Nazi Party was. On 24 February 1925 a mass inaugural meeting was held in Munich. Hitler spoke for 2 hours and his Bavarian sidekicks — who had been quarrelling bitterly among themselves — now swore loyalty to their leader and to the party. Munich was to continue as the site of the NSDAP headquarters. Hitler resisted all attempts to move it further north. But a real tension continued between the Bavarian headquarters of the party and the branches in northern Germany.

Hitler was also determined to bring the SA under greater control. This led to the resignation of Röhm and his replacement by Captain Franz von Pfeffer, a more amenable tool. A northern group of politicians, centred around **Gregor Strasser** and **Josef Goebbels**, was anxious to emphasise the socialist nature of the NSDAP. In foreign policy these men stressed the possibilities of cooperation with Bolshevik Russia and demanded a party commitment against the wealth and privileges of the former German princes. Hitler totally outmanoeuvred this group at a conference held at Bamberg in February 1926 by packing the meeting with his southern supporters. The young Goebbels was appalled, recording in his diary, 'I no longer believe fully in Hitler'. Yet 2 months later Hitler charmed him, winning him over totally. This time Goebbels wrote in his diary, 'Adolf Hitler, I love you because you are both great and simple at the same time'. Strasser was also won over and appointed propaganda chief at the end of the year. Goebbels was appointed party **Gauleiter** of Berlin, with the task of winning the capital for the NSDAP. Hitler's skill as a politician rested not only on his public speaking but also on his charisma and ability to manipulate other politicians.

It would be a mistake, however, to focus entirely on Hitler or even the other party bosses between 1925 and 1928. The importance of these years to the future triumph of the Nazi Party lay in the spread of 'local groups' throughout the whole of Weimar Germany. The establishment and success of these depended upon the energy and character of the individual Nazis in the area. Near Hanover, in the little town of **Northeim**, the Nazis owed much to the brutal energy of a local lad, Ernst Girmann, and the high moral character of the local bookseller, Wilhelm Spannaus — a pillar of the local community and church and one of the first to join the Nazi Party in the town. Many felt that if the Nazi Party was good enough for Spannaus, then it was good enough for them. Across Germany, party membership grew steadily from 27,000 at the end of 1925 to 108,000 in 1928. Although the typical party member was likely to be lower-middle-class and young, the party — unlike others — did transcend class and religious boundaries.

The task of the local group was propaganda, whether through pamphlets, meetings or face-to-face confrontation. From top to bottom the party appreciated the need to go out and convert, a feature that marked it almost as a religious movement. Money always remained a problem. Each local group had to fund its own activities as well as make a contribution to party headquarters in Munich. Subordinate special groups were created within the party, e.g. the National Socialist Union of University Students. A youth branch was created in 1926, when the words Hitler Youth appeared for the first time.

What was created between 1925 and 1928 was a formidable modern party political machine that could, when the time was right, capture political power. Unfortunately for Hitler and the Nazi Party, the time was not right. In the 1928 Reichstag election it gained only 810,000 votes and a mere 12 seats. This poor performance brought one unlooked-for blessing. Hitler's public speaking ban was lifted in Prussia and most other German states.

Glossary and concepts

Gauleiter — regional Nazi Party boss. Gauleiters have often been likened to medieval barons, enjoying wide local independence in return for their unconditional loyalty to the party leader.

Northeim — small town in central north Germany, near to Hanover and the subject of an excellent detailed study by the American William Sheridan Allen, who published his findings in a book entitled *The Nazi Seizure of Power* (1965, Franklin Watts, New York).

Key figures

Josef Goebbels (1897–1945) — a clever intellectual from a working-class Catholic background in western Germany. He joined the NSDAP in 1924 and was completely won over by Hitler's personality in 1926. Hitler sent him to Berlin to win the capital for the Nazis. He failed, but impressed many with his courage and energy. He was placed in charge of party propaganda in 1929 and masterminded the Nazi breakthrough in the election of September 1930. After Hitler came to power, Goebbels was appointed Minister of Enlightenment and Propaganda, a post he held until 1945. He committed suicide with his wife and six children at the same time as Hitler.

Gregor Strasser (1892–1934) — joined the Nazi Party in the early 1920s and took part in the Munich Putsch. He became leader of the north German wing of the party and favoured more radical, socialist policies. He was the original patron of Goebbels. He was an excellent administrator, and the second most important person in the party to Hitler until their quarrel in 1932. He withdrew from active politics but was murdered in 1934 in the Night of the Long Knives.

Gustav Stresemann (1878–1929) — leader of the DVP and a key figure in enabling the Weimar Republic to prosper during the years 1924–29. During these 5 years he was Foreign Minister and massively improved Germany's standing in the world. He was also crucial in holding together various coalitions. His death in October 1929 was a disaster for democracy in Germany.

The Nazi breakthrough to power, 1929–33

The death throes of the Weimar Republic

Most people associated the economic crisis that struck Germany in 1929 with the Wall Street Crash of October of that year. In fact the German economy was already in serious trouble. Agriculture in particular had been struggling for years. Over 13 million people owed their livelihoods directly to farming: a far larger proportion of the population than was the case in Britain. Agricultural protection, which had been in place since 1879, was removed in 1924 and foreign competition began to hurt many small and less efficient farmers. Bankruptcies multiplied and debts to banks increased. Grain prices fell after 1927 and there was serious distress. Early in 1928 there were widespread demonstrations by farmers in many regions. In Oldenburg 30,000 people demonstrated. In Schleswig-Holstein the number of protesters reached 140,000 and there was widespread violence. Rural suffering was keenly felt because farmers and farm labourers were not included in the National Insurance scheme of 1927. As farm incomes collapsed, misery and hunger became widespread. This became increasingly acute as depression settled over Germany between 1930 and 1931.

In urban and industrial Germany all was not well at the beginning of 1929. At the end of 1928 there had been a bitter dispute within the Ruhr steel industry over wages. Employers felt that wages were too high and that the government arbitration system favoured the workers. Many powerful industrialists in Weimar Germany were becoming disillusioned with the system. Growth was slowing down everywhere in 1929. The flow of foreign investment was decreasing before the Wall Street Crash. The slump in the USA was doubly disastrous for Germany. The influx of capital on which Germany relied disappeared and many companies found themselves called upon to repay their debts. Exports were also hit as Germany's foreign trade collapsed. Unemployment mounted. In 1929 it stood at 2 million; by 1931 it reached 4½ million. In that year there was a series of bank collapses that added to the country's woes. By 1932 unemployment had reached nearly 6 million and even this figure understated the scale of the problem. Many in agriculture were virtually unemployed, yet the statistics did not include these. At least a third of all working Germans were without wages. This amounted to a vast tide of human misery, which showed itself in the suicide statistics of 250 per million inhabitants (compared to 85 per million in Britain). Despair and fear stalked the land. Those who were unemployed worried about where the next crust of bread was going to come from and those who still had jobs were terrified that they would join the ranks of the unemployed.

A political crisis mirrored the economic one. Like the economic crisis, its origins pre-dated the Wall Street Crash of October 1929. Party politics was being polarised, making the cooperation that was essential to coalition government increasingly difficult to achieve. The Communist Party, under orders from Moscow, saw the SPD not as its natural ally but as its bitterest enemy, a rival for the working-class vote. The KPD constantly sniped at the moderate socialists, denouncing them as class traitors. This made it harder for the SPD to work with the bourgeois parties to achieve the consensus that was necessary for good government.

In December 1928 the Centre Party also moved over to the right when Monsignor Kaas won the leadership. The DDP, perhaps the party most loyal to the republic, was fading away. On the right, the DNVP — which, although openly monarchist, had at least increasingly cooperated with the other parties — came under the leadership of **Alfred Hugenberg** in October 1928. He wished to restructure the Weimar Republic on authoritarian grounds.

The crucial figure holding together the democratic coalition government was Gustav Stresemann, the Foreign Minister. In 1929 he pulled off a major triumph when he persuaded the British and French to accept a further reduction in reparations, which became known as the **Young Plan**. The Allies also agreed to withdraw all their troops from Germany 5 years early. It was Stresemann's last diplomatic achievement, as he died suddenly on 3 October 1929 at the age of 51. This was a severe blow to the Müller coalition government. Hugenberg launched a nationwide campaign against the Young Plan — a campaign into which he drew Hitler. A national referendum was held in December 1929. Only 13% voted for Hitler and Hugenberg's call to reject the plan. Hitler did not mind the defeat, because the campaign had given him enormous press coverage.

In March 1930 the economic crisis suddenly intensified the political crisis. Government revenue fell sharply as the slump began to bite, while at the same time expenditure rose rapidly, with the need to pay welfare benefits to the unemployed. In the light of prevailing orthodox economic theory, either taxation had to rise or benefits had to be cut. The SPD and the DVP could not agree a joint course of action. The middle-class DVP insisted on benefit cuts, which the SPD would not concede. The governing coalition broke up.

No chancellor could be found who could command a majority in the Reichstag. The President, Hindenburg, appointed a member of the Catholic Centre Party, **Heinrich Brüning**, as Chancellor and agreed that he would support Brüning's rule through the use of presidential emergency decrees. Parliamentary democracy had effectively come to an end — or it was, at the very least, suspended. In an attempt to gain a majority, Brüning held Reichstag elections in September 1930. These were a disaster for moderate politics. Both the extreme right and the extreme left made significant gains. Germany seemed to be fragmenting and becoming ungovernable. Street violence increased as the slump deepened. For 2 years Brüning wrestled with an almost impossible situation. His attempt to cut government expenditure arguably made the slump worse in the short term. In 1932 he persuaded the Allies to drop all reparations, but their agreement came too late to prevent his dismissal by President Hindenburg.

Hindenburg's coolness towards Brüning sprang in part from Brüning's own miscalculations. Brüning had persuaded the ageing Hindenburg to stand for re-election as President in 1932, telling him that it would be a walkover and would require little effort. Brüning was sadly mistaken and the elections went to a second ballot when Hindenburg failed to get an overall majority in the first. Brüning and Hindenburg also argued over measures to promote agricultural reform. The President refused to sign an emergency decree dealing with bankrupt agricultural estates in eastern Germany and Brüning was forced to resign.

Following Brüning's resignation, Hindenburg was persuaded to try to establish a majority conservative coalition government, thereby escaping the need for rule by presidential decree. A key figure in conservative circles was a clever political general called **Kurt von Schleicher**. He, like many army officers, was worried that Germany would disintegrate into civil war and that the army, instead of defending Germany from its foreign enemies, would have to take to the streets and risk killing German citizens in order to restore order. The President picked a charming aristocrat from the Centre Party, **Franz von Papen**, as his new Chancellor on 1 June 1932, in the hope that von Papen could do a deal with both the DNVP and the Nazis. Hitler's price for cooperation, which von Papen agreed to pay, was another general election. The Nazi vote soared and Hitler, in a stronger position than before, refused to serve under von Papen. The street violence intensified in the autumn and in desperation von Papen called fresh elections in November. The Nazi vote fell slightly but that of the communists increased.

Von Schleicher stepped in, persuading President Hindenburg to dismiss von Papen as Chancellor. Hindenburg appointed von Schleicher to replace von Papen. Von Schleicher hoped to achieve a left-wing coalition majority government by uniting the SPD with part of the Nazi Party under Gregor Strasser. The plan failed and the government continued relying on presidential emergency decree for its legality.

Von Papen was furious with von Schleicher and determined on revenge. Von Schleicher's failure provided him with his opportunity. After weeks of complex negotiations the ancient President was prevailed upon to accept Adolf Hitler as Chancellor in a coalition government with the DNVP. The conservatives like Hugenberg and von Papen thought they were using Hitler to achieve a more authoritarian system of government. He would be their front man. They would govern. They were mistaken.

The Nazi breakthrough to power

Before 1928 the Nazi Party had been essentially an urban party drawing its support from small craftsmen and young ex-soldiers. It had set itself the task of winning over the German working class and for this reason Goebbels had been sent to Berlin. On the whole it had not succeeded by 1928, as the general election results showed.

Despite the generally poor performance, however, there were encouraging signs that the party was doing well among the distressed farming community. In Oldenburg, where there had been extensive protest demonstrations by farmers, the Nazis picked up 7.5% of the vote in the Landtag elections of May 1928. They gradually decided to shift their efforts to winning the rural vote. The interests and needs of farmers began to be addressed in Nazi propaganda and eventually, in June 1930, the party created a special section to target farmers, under Walther Darre. The party organisations created to target youth were also beginning to have an effect and the Nazis were winning over large numbers of students at universities. In the course of 1929, Hitler's astute alliance with Hugenberg in a campaign against the Young Plan provided him with access to the mass media. Hugenberg owned several newspapers and a radio and film empire. Even though the vote was lost, Hitler gained a coverage throughout Germany that he would otherwise not have had. By the end of 1929 party membership had nearly doubled to 176,000, and the party received a very encouraging result in the Thuringia Landtag election, scoring just over 11% of the vote. As a result, for the first time, a Nazi became a regional minister. From being a fringe party that had no real political importance, the Nazis had reached a position whereby they had to be taken more seriously.

As the depression hit ever harder at Germans' pockets and self-confidence, the attraction of the Nazis increased. Farmers and young voters seem to have been particularly susceptible to the Nazi message. What marked the Nazi Party out was its appeal to all social groups and all religions, though it did less well in the traditional urban working-class centres and devout Catholic areas loyal to the Centre Party. Nonetheless, it did attract many workers and many Catholics. It could claim to be a truly national party and this was an essential part of its appeal. It promised to restore the unity after which many Germans hankered. It looked back to the spirit of 1914 and denounced the November Criminals of 1918. Jews, Marxists and the Treaty of Versailles were the stock-in-trade villains of the Nazis. They offered no precise solutions to the slump, simply asserting that the Weimar system had failed and should be replaced.

The evidence of Nazi popularity in the Saxony Landtag election was confirmed when Brüning mistakenly called a general election in September 1930. Hitler's party did spectacularly well, gaining 18% of the vote and 107 Reichstag seats. The Nazis became the second biggest party after the SPD. A return to democratic parliamentary government, which is what Brüning had hoped to achieve, was now almost impossible. In Northeim the Nazi vote increased from 123 to 1,742, 28% of the electorate. Of these, nearly half were new voters, either newly qualified or voters who had not bothered to vote before. Hitler was now a major national politician.

Street violence escalated as brutal confrontations between the NSDAP supporters and the communists became ever more frequent. The Nazis sought the communists out and made a hero out of Horst Wessel, who was shot in 1930 by a communist gunman. According to the communists, the killing arose from an argument over a retired prostitute, but Goebbels turned Horst Wessel into a religious martyr in the obituary that appeared in his paper, *Der Angriff*. Wessel, an SA man, had composed a battle song in 1929 and this now became the hymn of the Nazi movement.

The numbers in the SA grew dramatically in line with the economic crisis. Early in 1931 it had 88,000 members. By the end of the year it had 260,000. The relationship between the party and the SA had never been easy. It required considerable skill on Hitler's part to maintain control. Many SA men resented the party bureaucrats at Gau headquarters. They wanted to return to the violence of 1923, preferring a head-on assault on the Weimar Republic to the creeping pace of the ballot box.

In 1930 Hitler had been forced to take over the leadership of the SA himself to restore some sort of control over the Berlin SA organisation. A further crisis developed in 1931 — generally referred to as **Stennes' Revolt**. Walther Stennes was the leader of the SA in the eastern regions of Germany. Hitler had already tried to increase the loyalty of the SA by recalling Ernst Röhm as Chief of Staff in January 1930. Stennes' resentment, both of Hitler's leadership and his pursuit of the parliamentary path to power, led to open rebellion and attacks on Hitler in a party paper. Hitler fought back with considerable skill, offering the SA men of Berlin a choice between Stennes, a retired police sergeant, and himself, the potential saviour of Germany. Hitler emerged triumphant and restored Goebbels' authority in Berlin over a purged SA. Throughout 1931 and 1932 Hitler was forced into a very delicate balancing act. He had to keep the radicals of the SA happy with promises of change, but he also had to keep the flood of new middle-class Nazi voters happy with promises of stability and order. It was to reassure the middle class that Hitler formed a tactical alliance in the autumn of 1931 with Alfred Hugenberg of the DNVP and Franz Seldte, head of the veterans association, the **Stahlhelm** ('Steel Helmet'). This alliance was known as the National Opposition, or the **Harzburg Front**, on account of a massive rally held on 11 October at Bad Harzburg. Such flirtations with the conservative right were disliked by the radicals of the SA and the party. It was one of Hitler's greatest political achievements that he was able to persuade large numbers of Germans that the Nazis were both a party of the right and a party of the left. By the spring of 1932 membership of the party had reached 1 million. It was an astonishing achievement in such a short time.

Elections were commonplace in 1932: there were two for the presidency in the spring, regional elections and two elections for the Reichstag. In the presidential elections Hitler felt strong enough to challenge Hindenburg for the presidency. Hitler forced a second ballot, which the old Field Marshal won only with the support of the SPD and the Centre Party — support he resented. Hitler gained 13 million votes in all and won the support of large numbers of middle-class conservative voters. Elections kept the country in a ferment of political activity and violence. The Nazis caused much of the latter, but posed as the party that could stop it. The growing strength of the communists frightened middle-class voters, leading many to the Nazi Party as the lesser of two evils.

Following the violence carried out by the SA in the presidential elections, the new government successfully banned the SA. Hitler was forced to choose humiliating submission, hateful to the radicals in his party, or military confrontation with the government, which he knew he would lose. This was a major setback but, as on other occasions, circumstances came to Hitler's rescue. First the Minister of Defence, responsible for the ban on the SA, was sacked by the President. Then the Chancellor, Brüning, was replaced by von Papen. The new Chancellor sought to gain Hitler's support in order to achieve a majority in the Reichstag. Hitler played his hand well. He hinted that cooperation would be forthcoming if fresh elections were held and the ban on the SA was lifted. Hitler got his way.

The result was an electoral triumph for the Nazis. They won nearly 37% of the vote. The result was the product of many factors. Hitler was certainly a star turn, moving rapidly from town to town in whistle-stop tours. Goebbels was a propagandist of genius. But it was not merely the Nazi leaders who were responsible for success. In many towns and villages that had never seen Hitler the voters turned out in their hundreds and thousands to vote for the Nazis. It was the local Nazi stalwarts who brought in these voters. The Nazis were now the biggest party in Germany and, quite understandably, Hitler demanded to be made Chancellor. The President refused to consider such a proposition. Hitler was not a gentleman. He belonged on the wilder extremes of politics and would, Hindenburg feared, destabilise Germany further if he became Chancellor. There was stalemate.

Von Papen continued as Chancellor with an even smaller number of Reichstag votes behind him than Brüning. In desperation, in November 1932, he persuaded the President to call a further Reichstag election. The Nazi Party was, as usual, strapped for cash. Already there were the first signs of recovery in the economy; possibly Hitler was too late. The election showed a real fall in support and the number of Nazi MPs reduced from 230 to 196. But Communist Party support increased to 17%. This was to help Hitler. Fear of the Communist Party led many of the old élite, who intrinsically disliked Hitler, to accept him as a necessary evil. Such was probably the view of Hindenburg.

November was the make-or-break month for the future Führer. General von Schleicher tried to break up the Nazi Party and win over a large segment of its MPs under Gregor Strasser. Hitler was deeply depressed but Strasser refused to join a government without Hitler's blessing. The result was that von Schleicher continued to rely on the President's emergency decrees. He was, in fact, rapidly losing the President's confidence and that of the other senior generals in the army. They were increasingly worried at the prospect of civil war and wanted a chancellor with a majority. It was in these circumstances that Hitler was brought into government, just as his support was beginning to fail. Von Papen persuaded the President to appoint Hitler as Chancellor with himself as Vice Chancellor. The majority of the Cabinet were not Nazis. Von Papen and Hugenberg, Minister of Economics, thought they had captured Hitler for their own purposes. They would use him. The army gave the government its blessing. Only two other ministers were Nazis, but one of these controlled the police. The wild celebrating by the SA and party supporters on that night of 30 January 1933 should have given von Papen and the other conservatives cause for concern.

Glossary and concepts

Harzburg Front — loose political alliance of the NSDAP, DNVP and the *Stahlhelm* against the Brüning government in 1931. This seemed to align the Nazis with the conservative forces in Germany and was much criticised by radical Nazis, who took the socialist element in the party seriously.

Stahlhelm — association of First World War veteran soldiers, led by Franz Seldte.

Stennes' Revolt — challenge to Hitler's authority and that of Goebbels in Berlin in 1931 by a group of SA men led by Walther Stennes. He and the SA men resented the attempt to control their violence, which Hitler feared would upset the middle class, which was increasingly coming over to the Nazi Party. Tension remained despite Hitler's victory, a tension that was not to be resolved until the Night of the Long Knives in 1934.

Young Plan — scheme negotiated by Gustav Stresemann just before his death (in 1929) for the reduction of reparations payments. It was a major diplomatic success, but to the nationalist forces of the NSDAP and the DNVP it was a reminder of the humiliation of Versailles. The two parties formed an alliance to reject the scheme following a national referendum. The campaign against the Young Plan gave Hitler valuable media coverage, even though the referendum was lost.

Key figures

Heinrich Brüning (1885–1970) — served as an officer in the First World War and became an MP in 1924 for the Catholic Centre Party. He became Chancellor in March 1930 but had no majority in Parliament and had to rely on presidential decrees. He tried to cut government expenditure and this possibly added to unemployment. He was dismissed by the President just as he had seen through the worst of the slump. When Hitler came to power Brüning left Germany and emigrated to the USA.

Alfred Hugenberg (1865–1951) — rich German politician who controlled a vast media empire. He was a nationalist and opposed to the Weimar Republic. This led him to cooperate with the NSDAP in 1929, 1931 and in Hitler's government of 1933. He resigned from this government in June and thereafter played little part in politics.

Franz von Papen (1879–1969) — a Roman Catholic aristocrat and soldier, he was appointed Chancellor in 1932 in the hope of producing a right-wing coalition government with a majority. He failed to do a deal with Hitler in the summer of 1932 but eventually played a vital part in bringing Hitler to power in January 1933. He served as Vice Chancellor until 1934 but then lost power and was sent as ambassador to Vienna.

Kurt von Schleicher (1882–1934) — a professional soldier who became the political liaison officer of the army High Command. In 1932 he had considerable influence over the President and passed on the concerns of many generals about civil war and the dangers of the army being dragged into it. He tried on two occasions to produce a majority government and in both cases failed. His failure opened the way for Hitler to come to power, but he never lost his taste for intrigue. This caused him to be shot in June 1934.

The consolidation of power, January–March 1933

From Chancellor to Führer

Hitler had become Chancellor on 30 January 1933. He was not, however, a dictator. He could be dismissed at any time by the President, and a majority of his Cabinet colleagues were not of his party. In many ways his appointment as Chancellor marked a return to democracy. It was yet another attempt to return to a government that could enjoy majority support in Parliament rather than depending on emergency presidential decree. The situation had changed dramatically by the end of March 1933, when it was clear that Hitler was not merely the dupe of those conservative politicians who had 'levered him into power'. Hitler's consolidation of power was not, of course, complete in March. His policy of *Gleichschaltung* (coordination) would extend up to and beyond August 1934, when Hitler combined the roles of Chancellor and President.

Inevitably, the focus of most narratives tends to be on Hitler and events in Berlin, but it should be noted that the consolidation going on at ground level in every town and region of Germany was just as important. Thousands of local enthusiasts strengthened the Nazi hold on town halls and regional government. It was this popular dynamic that made the consolidation of power so effective and made it impossible for the conservatives around Hitler in Berlin to resist.

Hitler's first move was to persuade the President to accept another election, which was fixed for March 1933. Hitler reassured the army chiefs in a meeting on 3 February. He promised them money for rearmament and — most important for the majority of them — their independence from politics. They would not be called upon to deal with the communists and could be allowed to focus on the business of expansion and rearmament. Many of the generals found Hitler vulgar, but they accepted the deal. General von Blomburg, as Minister of War, was reassuring to them. On 20 February another important meeting was held with the chiefs of industry, who were reassured that capitalism was safe under the Nazis — in fact even safer than before, for Marxists would be dealt with. At the end of the meeting 3 million marks were promised for the election campaign. Perhaps even more important than these deals with the rich and powerful was the insidious perversion of the police. Already in 1932, under von Papen, a purge of senior police officers had begun. Now, under Goering and Frick, this was carried much further. On 17 February Goering urged the police to cooperate with the SA and use every form of violence against the communists, including firearms. On 22 February 50,000 SA men were drafted into the police as auxiliaries. The police would no longer be neutral when it came to breaking up demonstrations and political meetings.

The political temperature was dramatically raised on the evening of 27 February 1933, when the Reichstag building burst into flames as a result of an arson attack by the 24-year-old Dutchman Marinus van der Lubbe. Van der Lubbe had once been a communist, and the Nazi leaders chose to believe that this was all part of a great communist plot to seize power. The blaze at the Parliament building, they claimed, was the signal for a communist uprising. There has been much debate among historians about this event. Some have tried to show that it was organised by the Nazis, but most modern research indicates that it was a fortuitous event that played into Hitler's hands. He and the other Nazi leaders appeared to be genuinely surprised by the blaze and acted as if they believed a Bolshevik seizure of power was imminent. Given Hitler's obsession with the communist rising in Munich in 1919, his outrage was probably genuine. The importance of this event lies in the use that was made of it. The President was persuaded to issue an emergency decree on 28 February 'for the protection of people and state'. Personal liberties were suspended and wide powers of arrest were granted to the government. The powers of the regional governments could be overridden. By the end of March 25,000 had been arrested in Prussia alone. The detainees were mainly communists, but some members of the SPD were also arrested. Many of the detained communists were held in temporary prisons where they were brutally tortured. The way had been opened for dictatorship.

In this frenzied atmosphere the last democratic elections in Weimar Germany were held on 5 March 1933. Despite the intimidation and the weighty government propaganda orchestrated by Goebbels, the government enjoyed only limited success. The Nazi vote rose to nearly 44%, which, together with the 8% for the DNVP, gave the government a clear majority. The result, though, was far short of the two-thirds majority that Hitler expected and needed to alter the constitution. As it happened, this did not matter. SA violence multiplied. To many it seemed Germany had been given over to hooligans. Party activists seized power throughout the country. Everywhere the Nazis took over the regional and city governments. In Bavaria, as was appropriate for the home of the movement, particularly vicious and enthusiastic Nazis gained control. Himmler, the head of the **Schutzstaffel** (SS), Hitler's personal bodyguard, became police chief and outdid Goering in his enthusiasm for the arrest and re-education of opponents of the regime.

Between 21 and 23 March 1933 three crucial developments signalled the future that awaited Germany. On 21 March a solemn piece of propaganda theatre was played out at Potsdam, the little town outside Berlin that has always been associated with the glories of Frederick the Great. President Hindenburg, in the full uniform of a

Prussian field marshal, partnered the new Reich Chancellor in a ceremony of national reconciliation and awakening. Old and new were to be bound together, creating the **Volksgemeinschaft**. The next day, far to the south in Bavaria, a new institution opened for the first time — Dachau, Himmler's new model concentration camp. It was a name that was to strike terror into many Germans over the next 12 years. On 23 March, at the first meeting of the new Reichstag in the Kroll Opera House in Berlin, the German Parliament passed what has become known as the Enabling Act. Its official name was the 'Act for the Removal of Distress from the People and the Reich'. After much debate the Centre Party agreed to support the Nazi Party, hoping to preserve the influence of the Catholic Church in the new Germany. Only 94 brave SPD deputies voted against the Bill. The Parliament transferred its authority for 4 years to the Chancellor. Weimar Germany had committed suicide.

Conclusions

Historians have argued for years over the fate of the Weimar Republic and the reasons for the triumph of Adolf Hitler. In postwar communist East Germany the standard explanation was that Hitler was merely the tool of threatened capitalists. Big business had put Hitler into power to crush the workers. In West Germany it was fashionable to explain the triumph of the Nazis in terms of Hitler's charismatic powers. It was as if Hitler had bewitched the country, and it is impossible to ignore his role. He was in many ways a politician of genius, an outstanding speaker, a superb manipulator of others; he also possessed a crucial sense of timing. Alongside Hitler, Goebbels must rank as one of the great propagandists of all time. Hitler certainly appreciated Goebbels' talents and he deserves much of the credit for the Nazi breakthrough in the election of 1930, which he managed for the party.

Yet the actions of these outstanding individuals do not explain the transformation of the Nazi Party between 1928, when it was little more than a fringe organisation, and 1932, when it had become a mass party. Clearly the economic slump and attendant misery created the right conditions for breakthrough. Poverty-stricken unemployed workers joined the Nazis in the hope of a better world. So did the young in their thousands; so did the peasants and so did the middle class, fearful of the Communist Party. The Nazi Party and Hitler filled a void that had been growing since the nineteenth century. It offered faith and hope to a world where traditional religion seemed less and less relevant. It was in many ways an alternative religious cult — with Hitler a cult leader. It offered order to a country that had lost its Kaiser. It offered redemption to a Germany that had been humiliated in 1919 and seen its currency disappear in 1923. The old world had been mocked in the 1920s by the radical artists and dramatists of the Weimar Republic but, in destroying the remnants of the old world, they had prepared the ground for new beliefs and new icons.

Ordinary Germans put Hitler into power. Large numbers never voted for him, but he was a popular politician who enjoyed support throughout all classes and regions of the country. Intelligence and education offered no immunity. The Nazi Party was filled with doctors of philosophy. Like most religions and cults, the Nazis' success had a strong theatrical element. The young Hitler had been obsessed with Wagner's grandiose operas. He saw himself in a Wagnerian role, saving Germany from Jewish and Marxist monsters. If only more Germans had laughed at the fantasy; Hitler was morbidly frightened of ridicule and perhaps secretly sensed his vulnerability. Not enough Germans laughed, but then there was little to make them laugh in 1932.

Glossary and concepts

Gleichschaltung **(forcible coordination)** — the Nazification of German political and social institutions. At the higher level this refers to the taking over of the *Länder*, or state governments, but it could involve the Nazification of, for example, a town choir or chess club, as happened in Northeim.

Schutzstaffel **(SS)** — originally a branch of the SA, the SS was founded in 1925 to protect leading Nazis at meetings. The uniform was black and not brown (as with the SA). Himmler was appointed its commander in 1929 and built it into the most formidable of all the subordinate organisations of Nazi Germany.

Volksgemeinschaft **(racial folk community)** — term to describe the vision of a harmonious Germany, devoid of class tensions and 'racial impurities'.

Questions & Answers

In this section there are three specimen exam questions. They illustrate the range and type of source extracts you will come across.

Two specimen answers are given to each exam question. One of these is an A-grade answer, but examples of lower-grade answers are included to point out common errors — either in approach or in exam technique.

All the specimen answers are the subject of detailed examiner comments, preceded by the icon ℓ. These should be studied carefully as they show how and why marks are awarded or lost. They demonstrate common features in A-grade answers such as:
- the appropriate use of outside knowledge to put source material in context
- a clear and persistent focus on answering the question asked
- a structured and logical approach
- an apportionment of time and effort within answers appropriate to marks that can be gained in different parts of the question

When exam papers are marked, all answers are given a level of response and then a precise numerical mark. Answers to questions worth 20 marks are normally marked to three levels:
- **level 1:** 1–6 marks
- **level 2:** 7–16 marks
- **level 3:** 17–20 marks

Answers to questions worth 40 marks are marked to four levels:
- **level 1:** 1–8 marks, involves very simple statements and the use of either own knowledge or information from one extract
- **level 2:** 9–20 marks, involves either own knowledge and limited source use, or excellent use of the sources alone, or excellent own knowledge
- **level 3:** 21–35 marks, involves using both sources and own knowledge with real focus on the question asked
- **level 4:** 36–40 marks, involves a sustained argument from both the sources and own knowledge

Question 1

Source 1: *From an account of a Nazi meeting in 1932 written at the time by a Hamburg school teacher*

When this speech was over, there was roaring enthusiasm and applause. Hitler saluted, gave his thanks, the Horst Wessel song sounded out across the course. Hitler was helped into his coat. Then he went — how many look up to him with a touching faith! As their helper, a saviour, their deliverer from unbearable distress — to him who rescues the Prussian prince, the scholar, the clergyman, the farmer, the worker, the unemployed, who rescues them, from the parties back into the nation.

Source 2: *From* Inside the Third Reich *by Albert Speer, later one of Hitler's ministers. He is writing about 1931 but the book was written many years later in the 1960s*

It must have been during these months that my mother saw an SA parade in the streets of Heidelberg. The sight of discipline in a time of chaos, the impression of energy in an atmosphere of universal hopelessness, seems to have won her over also. At any rate, without ever having heard a speech or read a pamphlet she joined the party. Both of us seem to have felt this decision to be a breach with a liberal family tradition. In any case we concealed it from one another and from my father. Only years later, long after I had become a part of Hitler's inner circle, did my mother and I discover by chance that we shared an early membership in the party.

Source 3: *From* Darkness over Germany *by E. Buller, published in 1941 but telling the story of a young German in 1931*

At the end of my time in university, I was unemployed for a year so I went back to do some research work in the hope that perhaps times would improve. But for five years I remained unemployed and I was broken in body and spirit and I learnt how stupid all my dreams were in those hard days at the university. I was not wanted by Germany, and certainly if I was not wanted here I was not wanted anywhere in the world.... Just then I was introduced to Hitler. You don't understand and I cannot explain either because I don't know what happened. But life for me took on a tremendous new significance. After all, Germany would rise again; after all, I was wanted. I've since committed myself, body soul and spirit to this movement for the resurrection of Germany.

question

Source 4: *Chancellors of the Weimar Republic, 1919–33, with names of parties forming the government*

Scheidemann, February–June 1919 (SPD, Centre, DDP)
Bauer, June 1919–March 1920 (SPD, Centre, DDP)
Müller, March–June 1920 (SPD, DDP, Centre)
Fehrenbach, June 1920–May 1921 (DDP, Centre, DVP)
Wirth, May–October 1921 (SPD, DDP, Centre)
Wirth, October 1921–November 1922 (SPD, DDP, Centre)
Cuno, November 1922–August 1923 (DDP, Centre, DVP)
Stresemann, August–October 1923 (SPD, DDP, Centre, DVP)
Stresemann, October–November 1923 (SPD to 3 November, DDP, Centre, DVP)
Marx, November 1923–June 1924 (DDP, Centre, BVP, DVP)
Marx, June 1924–January 1925 (DDP, Centre, DVP)
Luther, January–December 1925 (Centre, DVP, DNVP, BVP)
Luther, January–May 1926 (Centre, DDP, DVP, BVP)
Marx, May–December 1926 (DDP, Centre, DVP, BVP)
Marx, January 1927–June 1928 (Centre, DVP, DNVP, BVP)
Müller, June 1928–March 1930 (SPD, DDP, Centre, BVP, DVP)
Brüning, March 1930–October 1931 (Presidential Cabinet)
Brüning, October 1931–May 1932 (Presidential Cabinet)
Von Papen, June–December 1932 (Presidential Cabinet)
Von Schleicher, December 1932–January 1933 (Presidential Cabinet)
Hitler, January 1933

Source 5: *From* Hitler and Nazi Germany *by Stephen J. Lee, 1998*

The rise of Hitler depended directly on the vulnerability of the Weimar Republic. Although in many respects an advanced democracy, the Republic was politically flawed and susceptible to economic crisis. There were practical difficulties arising out of the constitution. Proportional representation, without a threshold, produced a multiplicity of parties, encouraged splinter groups and made coalition governments inevitable, with all the potential for internal disagreement which these so often carry. This was made worse at certain points in the history of the Republic by economic crises, especially those of 1921–23 and 1929–31. The collapse of democracy in 1929 was due to the interaction of the two processes. The Great Coalition — which comprised the Social Democratic Party (SPD), the Centre, the People's Party (DVP) and the Democratic Party (DDP) — was already in disarray before 1929 but was brought down by the disagreement between the SPD and the Centre for proposals to cut unemployment benefit. The results were the decline of party politics and the growth of authoritarian government with less and less recourse to the Reichstag. As will be seen, this was an ideal situation for the Nazi Party.

(a) Study Sources 1, 2 and 3.

How far do these three sources support the view that Hitler was the crucial factor in attracting supporters to the Nazi Party in 1931–32? (20 marks)

(b) Study Sources 4 and 5 and use your own knowledge.

How important was the nature of the Weimar Constitution in explaining the growth in support for the Nazi Party in the years 1928–30? (40 marks)

Answer to question 1: candidate A

(a) All three sources relate to the years in question and all three extracts are concerned with the reasons why four individuals joined the Nazi Party. Sources 1 and 3 clearly place Hitler as a central cause. Source 1 describes the 'roaring enthusiasm and applause' and talks of him as a saviour appealing to all levels of German society. Source 3 also places Hitler centrally in the conversion process with the sentence 'Just then I was introduced to Hitler', implying his responsibility. In this sense both sources support the notion of Hitler's vital importance in attracting support.

Source 2, on the other hand, can be used to contradict this proposition. Speer's mother joined the party 'without ever having heard a speech' and it was the sight of a disciplined SA parade that appears to have been the crucial factor. Hitler was therefore only a distant influence, which is not discussed.

All three sources do, however, suggest another crucial factor, namely the economic depression. There is talk in Source 1 of deliverance from 'unbearable distress'. Source 2 mentions 'universal hopelessness' and the author of Source 3 refers to his despair at being unwanted and unemployed. In this sense the slump and social crisis was the crucial factor in all three sources.

(b) 'An ideal situation for the Nazi Party' is Source 5's comment on the situation in 1929–30. The electoral facts bear this out. In 1928 the NSDAP had only 12 deputies in the Reichstag, but in September 1930 they secured over 18% of the votes cast, making the Nazis the second biggest party with 107 seats.

According to Source 5, this ideal situation was due to the collapse of democracy in 1929–30, brought about by two contributory factors: economic crisis and political instability. The two converged in 1929 in peculiar circumstances, which destroyed the coalition government. Weimar Germany had operated on a system of proportional representation, which led to the formation of many different parties and thus to the necessity of coalition governments, which were inherently unstable and prone to division. Source 5 asserts that there were 'practical difficulties' arising out of the Weimar Constitution. This was largely a result of proportional representation, which created many parties and splinter groups within the Reichstag. As it was extremely unlikely that any party would ever gain an overall majority, governments were, by necessity, formed through coalition. They were therefore constantly prone to internal disagreement and collapse. Source 4 shows a list of

Weimar chancellors from 1919 to 1933, alongside the parties comprising the coalition government at the time. It supports the ideas expressed in Source 5 in that it illustrates that a government, and particularly a chancellor, often lasted little more than a few months. Indeed, there were 20 governments formed in only 14 years. This obviously suggests unstable government, constant disagreement and a lack of coherent policy. Only Müller and the 'Great Coalition' of 1928–30, which consisted of five different parties, existed for almost 2 years. Brüning lasted a similar length of time, but under a far more authoritarian government controlled by presidential cabinet.

Source 5 asserts, therefore, that the Weimar Constitution posed real practical difficulties, as the Weimar government clearly exhibited constant fluctuation and inconstancy and led to popular disillusionment with the Weimar Republic, on which the Nazis played. There was a demand for a more authoritarian form of government. The system of proportional representation also helped the NSDAP establish itself, as it gave representation to smaller parties.

The economic crisis of 1929–33 was also a vital factor in the growth of Nazi support, largely because it weakened the existing government and led to a political crisis. The economic crisis beginning in 1929 posed serious difficulties for Chancellor Müller and the coalition government in power. The slow economic recovery from the dark days of hyperinflation in the early 1920s was rapidly reversed as the cash from the USA that was backing this recovery dried up. Banks closed, industrial production fell by 42% and the farming community was hit particularly hard. Unemployment rose dramatically and continued to do so, reaching nearly 30% by 1932. As Source 5 indicates, such economic difficulties had political consequences. Budgetary arguments split the coalition, which was brought down over disagreement about the cutting of unemployment benefit. The political climate was therefore one of fragmentation and disarray, while the economic slump impacted on the daily lives of the population. It was most obvious among rural peasant farmers, who comprised an important 30% of the population. They had suffered as a result of agricultural depression and threw their support behind the Nazis.

It is, however, also important to recognise the strengths of the Nazi Party, and Hitler in particular. The increase in Nazi support was the result not only of a negative response to unfavourable circumstances, but also of positive Nazi action. The Nazi Party launched a particularly vigorous campaign in the countryside, where they successfully infiltrated rural organisations and were rewarded with extensive support. Nazi scaremongering and tireless campaigns against the Communists were also successful in luring a large proportion of the middle classes into the fold. The Nazis could offer law and order in the face of the Communist threat and a return to the 'golden era' before the instability of Weimar democracy.

First-time voters and the young also responded to the Nazi rallying cry. The Nazis were new, untainted with failure and possessed enthusiasm, which had great appeal. Hitler's own personal allure should also be emphasised. His tremendous oratorical ability and shrewd political rhetoric helped cement the broad Nazi appeal. Thus, while he may have been helped by the economic crisis and the political situation provoked by the nature of the Weimar Constitution, Hitler was able to seize opportunities and ensure the rapid expansion of Nazi support in the years 1928–30. The same constitution had been in operation since 1919, but the Nazi breakthrough only took place 10 years later. A coming together of many factors explains this.

e The response to part (a) is of high quality and well written, making full and effective use of all three sources. Clear cross-referencing takes place and points are supported with apposite quotations. The attributions provided are also used appropriately. There is a sharp focus on the question set and the candidate never resorts to extraneous own knowledge. This response would be awarded level 3: 20 (full) marks.

The response to part (b) is well informed and shows a constant capacity to focus on the question asked and use the sources, which drive the answer rather than being simply bolted on as an afterthought. This response would gain level 4: 38 marks.

Overall, this response would obtain an A grade.

■ ■ ■

Answer to question 1: candidate B

(a) Source 1 records the experience of a Hamburg schoolteacher at a Nazi meeting in 1932. It shows how important the figure of Hitler was in himself. It describes how taken in both the teacher and the crowd were with him, and how he seemed to them to be a saviour to people in all walks of life. Source 2 shows how important the discipline of the Nazi Party was when everything seemed to be in chaos. So the source explains that the image of authority provided a feeling of stability when chaos prevailed. In this sense it is very useful to the historian in terms of reconstructing a picture of Hitler's rise to power but does not say much about Hitler's role in contrast to both of the other sources. The third source, like the first one, makes much of Hitler as the key to winning over the convert. So, in conclusion, the first and the last source agree on the importance of Hitler but the second does not.

(b) The decline of democracy in 1929 in Weimar Germany occurred for a series of reasons. A part of the problem was Hindenburg's use of Article 48, which granted him great power and undermined democracy. This was not helped by the tradition of authority that existed before Weimar Germany, since people held on to a faith in strong leadership. Also, the political system of proportional representation undermined democracy because it led to coalition governments. Besides this, there was also a big economic problem in Weimar Germany in the late 1920s when America called in loans organised under Gustav Stresemann, therefore damaging faith in the system. Source 5 points out the problem with coalition governments, wedded to the economic crisis, providing a good basis for the Nazis' success.

Source 4 gives a list of chancellors of the Weimar Republic from 1919 to 1933 and shows that throughout the whole period of the Weimar Republic every government was a coalition of at least three parties. It also shows how the republic gradually became more right-wing. In the early 1920s the biggest parties were the SPD and the Centre, but by the late 1920s the nationalists became more powerful, until Brüning (a nationalist) eventually took over. Source 5 shows how the Weimar Constitution was politically flawed, with the system of proportional representation leading to coalition governments, making efficient government of the country difficult. It also explains how the DVP and the DDP, which formed the Great Coalition, were broken by the disagreement over cutting unemployment benefit. This, it argues, paved the way for the Nazis. In this way Source 4 does support Source 5, since it shows the growth of the right wing just as the DVP and the DDP were splitting up.

The economic crisis of 1929 to 1933 in Germany grew out of the Wall Street Crash in America. As an aspect of the growth in support for the Nazi Party it is very important. Yet it alone cannot explain the Nazis' success. Germany in 1919 to 1923 was politically fragile, owing to the problem of resentment that persisted among the army following the end of the First World War. Also, the hyperinflation of 1923 created more hostility towards the politics of the day. The impact of this instability was to live in the memory of the German nation, in spite of the increased prosperity of the years from 1924 to 1929. The early years of the Weimar Constitution had other problems, which came to the fore at the end of the decade. One of these problems was that of Article 48, which granted the president excessive power and, although the first president of Weimar, Friedrich Ebert, made little use of this, his successor, Hindenburg, did. Also, there was a strong tradition of authoritarianism in German politics, and many hankered after a return to the pre-war situation.

Nevertheless, the concerns of the German nation were temporarily reduced in the 1925–29 period when, under Gustav Stresemann, the economic problems were cured by taking out loans from America. However, a problem that exploded in 1930 was with the system of proportional representation, which led to coalition governments, as Source 4 shows. Fortunately, as long as the coalition could agree on certain matters, problems could be kept to a minimum. Yet in 1930 the most solid coalition, made up of the SPD, the DVP and the Centre Party, fell apart, and, from that point on, each chancellor was chosen by Hindenburg. This happened at the same time as the German economy collapsed. Because of the Wall Street Crash this meant that no more loans could be taken out, and also that those already taken were recalled. Because of this, unemployment rose to 6 million by 1932 and industrial production fell by 42%. Also, the economic depression affected the agricultural industry and so rural Germany was badly affected as well. No doubt because of these problems, the people were looking for a solution elsewhere, their questions & answers

faith in the dominant parties having been destroyed. Because of this, it is not surprising that support for the Nazi Party grew.

e This response to part (a) is not as good as the A-grade candidate's. It is not as well constructed and gives the impression of a mechanical summary of the sources, almost answering the question incidentally. A basic comparison is made, which enables the answer to reach level 2: 7 marks.

The answer to part (b) is not as well structured or expressed as the A-grade candidate's, and this is illustrated by the tendency to be repetitious. Both sources are used and there is plenty of accurate and relevant own knowledge, but the answer is not driven by the sources, which tend to be used almost as afterthoughts. This answer would attain a low level 3: 22 marks.

Question 2

Source 1: *From* Mein Kampf *by Adolf Hitler, written in 1924 but writing about 1914, when he became a frontline soldier*

And then came a damp, cold night in Flanders, through which we marched in silence, and when the day began to emerge from the mists suddenly an iron greeting came whizzing at us over our heads, and with a sharp report sent the little pellets flying between our ranks, ripping up the wet ground; but even before the little cloud had passed, from 200 throats the first cheer arose to meet the first messenger of death. Then a crackling and a roaring, a singing and a howling began, and with feverish eyes each one of us was drawn forward, faster and faster, and suddenly past field and hedges the fight began, the fight of man against man. And from the distance the strains of a song reached our ears, coming closer and closer, leaping from company to company, and just as death plunged a busy hand into our ranks the song reached us too and we passed it along: Deutschland, Deutschland über Alles ['Germany Over All' — the national anthem]. Four days later we came back. Even our step had changed. 17-year-old boys now looked like men.

Source 2: *From* The Spirit of 1914 *by Kurt Tucholsky, written in 1924*

The wave of drunkenness which overtook the country ten years ago has left behind many hung-over people, who know no other cure for their hangover than to become drunk again. They have learned nothing.

Today the spiritual foundation on which Germany rests is no different from that when it was founded. No spiritual experience has touched the country, for the war was none. It changed bodies into corpses, but it left the spirit completely untouched.

Source 3: *From* Fire *by Ernst Junger, written in 1922 on the basis of his wartime experiences as a soldier*

In the neighbouring regiment on the left there bursts a storm of fire. It is a feinting maneuver, to confuse and split enemy artillery. It is just about time. Now the task is to gather oneself. Yes, it is perhaps a pity. Perhaps as well we are sacrificing ourselves for something inessential. But no one can rob us of our value. Essential is not what we are fighting for, but how we fight. Onward towards the goal, until we triumph or are left behind. The warriors' spirit, the exposure of oneself to risk, even for the tiniest idea, weighs more heavily in the scale than all the brooding about good and evil. We want to show what we have in us; then, if we fall, we will truly have lived to the full.

Source 4: *From the evidence given by Franz von Papen at his trial in Nuremberg published in 1946 but referring to the events of 1933*

Further support of the von Schleicher presidential cabinet by means of a declaration of a state of emergency and the suspension of Parliament, which was against the constitution, had been rejected by the Reich President on the 23rd. He rejected these proposals — as we know, von Schleicher had told him in December that a violation of the constitution would mean civil war and a civil war would mean chaos — because he said I am not in a position with the army and with the police to maintain law and order. Since Hitler offered to participate in a presidential cabinet, this was the only remaining possibility and all the forces and political parties which supported my government in 1932 were available for this.

Q. What were the instructions which the Reich President gave you?

A. The instructions given me by von Hindenburg were as follows: the formation of a government under the leadership of Hitler, with the utmost restriction of National Socialist influence and within the framework of the constitution.

Source 5: *From* Germans into Nazis *by Peter Fritzsche, written in 1998*

National Socialists captured the political imagination of almost one in every two voters because they challenged the authoritarian legacy of the Empire, rejected the class-based convictions of Social Democrats and Communists, and both honoured the solidarity and upheld the patriotism of the nation at war. They thus twisted together strands from the political left and the political right, without being loyal to the beliefs of either camp. Mobilising enormous energy and profound expectation for a new beginning, re-imagining the nation as a fiercely nationalistic body politic, and willing to bloody the streets to realise their aims, the Nazis seized power in January 1933 in what amounted to a national revolution.

(a) **Study Sources 1, 2 and 3.**
How far do these sources agree in their attitudes to the First World War? (20 marks)
(b) **Study Sources 4 and 5 and use your own knowledge.**
How important was the threat of violence by Nazis in their gaining of power in 1933?

(40 marks)

■ ■ ■

Answer to question 2: candidate A

(a) The three sources all come from the early 1920s but take different approaches to the recent conflict. Source 1 is essentially positive about the experience of war, despite the references to the discomfort and danger of war — 'damp, cold night', 'first messenger of death' etc. The key is the emphasis on patriotism and the transforming of boys into 'real men'. This contrasts totally with the second source, which mentions only the changing of 'bodies into corpses'. This source seems to see the war in a wholly negative way, as a bout of drunken stupor that has brought nothing of value, merely leaving a 'hangover'. The last source has some points of similarity to Source 1, conveying the excitement of battle despite the risks of death. There seems to be none of Source 1's patriotism, however, and the source hints that the war is futile or, as it calls it, 'inessential'. But it does see war as living life to the full. Action, the author seems to believe, is better than 'brooding about good and evil', even if the action is not strictly necessary. All three, therefore, are different, but Sources 1 and 3, written from soldiers' perspectives, share some positive views. There is nothing to suggest that Source 2 was written by an ex-soldier and this may explain its negative approach to the war.

(b) Source 5 refers to the Nazis' willingness to 'bloody the streets', and the phrase 'seized power' implies violence. Source 4, however, despite the reference to 'civil war', describes the process that brought Hitler to power as chancellor in January 1933 and refers to it as 'within the framework of the constitution'. Violence was a part of the Nazi strategy, but so was the ballot box and political negotiation.

The NSDAP had a paramilitary force, the SA, which could be used to disrupt the meetings of rival parties and intimidate opponents. Communists in particular were targeted and pitched battles took place in some of the larger industrial cities such as Berlin. In Source 4 the chancellor at the time, von Schleicher, speaks of the threat of civil war that the rival paramilitaries posed. He felt that in January 1933 there was a threat of chaos and that the government could not control both the Nazis and the Communists with the small army and the police. In this sense, violence played a part in persuading the president to opt for Hitler, and in allowing the Nazis to campaign for votes. It was to play an even bigger part in the consolidation of Nazi power after January.

However, as Source 5 indicates, it was the fact that the Nazis enjoyed widespread support that was crucial — 'almost one in every two voters'. In the July 1932 Reichstag elections, the NSDAP had gained 36% of the vote. After the failure of the Munich Putsch in 1923, Hitler had rejected the armed seizure of power and opted for the ballot box. He had had some difficulty in controlling the SA from time to time, but he showed a determination to avoid confrontation with the army and preferred to gain power legally. This was essential in view of the increasing middle-class support the party attracted as a result of fear of the Communists. Despite this, they still attracted much support from the young working class and the rural poor. The Nazis were unique as a party and, as Source 5 says, they rejected the 'class-based convictions of Social Democrats and Communists'. It was this broad support that enabled von Papen to persuade Hindenburg to accept Hitler as chancellor, a process described in Source 4 and, as it indicates, it was 'within the framework of the constitution'. Hitler thus came to power not as a result of an armed coup, but as a result of a political deal of the sort that had taken place before the formation of every other Weimar coalition government.

The Nazis had used violence at times and they certainly used it extensively later in 1933 but, despite the willingness to 'bloody the streets', it was their success at the ballot box combined with the willingness of politicians like von Papen to work with them that brought them to power.

🄔 The response to part (a) is excellent, with a clear comparison made, drawing out points of contrast and similarities and supporting these with appropriate quotations. The attributions are also brought into play. At no point does the candidate stray outside the sources for support. This response would be awarded level 3: 19 marks.

The response to part (b) is focused tightly on the question and effectively deploys the sources and own knowledge. As the first paragraph indicates, it is an answer driven by the sources, which are constantly referred to throughout the essay. There is debate, adequate own knowledge and a short conclusion. The response, despite its brevity, would be awarded level 4: 37 marks.

■ ■ ■

Answer to question 2: candidate B

(a) Source 1 is by Adolf Hitler and although it makes reference to death and destruction, it is largely positive about the experience of conflict, which it feels has turned boys into men after 4 days. Source 2 is very different. It likens the war to a bout of drunkenness, which has simply left the country with a massive hangover. It says nothing positive about the war, in sharp contrast to the first source. The third source is more complicated in its attitudes. It recognises the threat of death and even hints that the war may be futile (inessential) in its aims but it suggests that it is exciting and gives people a chance to prove themselves.

(b) The Nazis clearly demonstrated that they were willing to use violence, but it was to be just one of the factors in Hitler's rise to power. By the end of March, Hitler was chancellor and the Nazis, in coalition with the National People's Party in 1933, enjoyed a majority in the Reichstag. This was the result of more than mere brute force.

The SA were responsible for most of the violence committed in the name of the Nazi Party. Indeed, it seemed to be their main, if unofficial, function. Violence of this type became noticeably acute during the 1933 election. Communist Party meetings and Social Democrat rallies were broken up, and violent street fights erupted. Even the more moderate Catholic Centre Party had its meetings disrupted. Many Communists had already been attacked or arrested in the wake of the Reichstag fire of February 1933. A Communist suspect confessed and Hitler used the fire as an excuse to pass a decree 'for the protection of people and state' which gave him emergency powers to place political opponents in custody. This led to 'authorised' violence as opponents of the Nazis were targeted, and demonstrates a clear willingness to use force. Indeed, this use of force appears to have been part of Nazi culture. Ultimately, as Source 5 claims, the Nazis were not afraid to 'bloody the streets', and this determination was an important factor in their success.

It should, however, be remembered that violence alone did not enable the Nazis to gain power. Germany, in early 1933, was still officially a democracy and Hitler needed to win votes. That he was able to do so impressively (the Nazis gained 43.9% of the vote in the March elections) owed something to the use of force, but also to political skill and popular appeal. As Source 5 claims, the Nazis could appeal effectively to members of both the left and right, by combining elements of both and emphasising the nationalistic element of the party, which was to prove a unifying factor. They played to the fears and requirements of particular groups with skill, capitalising for example on the middle-class fear of communism. The party was also successful with first-time voters and the young. It was the party of youth and energy, offering hope of a new age. The Nazis had an effective campaigning machine capable of targeting certain groups. As Source 5 states, they were able to capture almost one in every two voters, an achievement that owed a great deal to clever politics and an effective party machine.

It should also be noted that the Nazis made the most of favourable circumstances. The economic slump of 1929–31 led to depression and unemployment, enabling the Nazis to tailor appeals to the disaffected, as they did successfully with peasant farmers, and to present themselves as a party of order and vitality in a time of chaos and disillusionment. The slump also led to the downfall of the coalition government in 1930, creating political uncertainty and setting a precedent for more authoritarian rule. In this climate, Hitler was appointed by President Hindenburg to the position of chancellor, as indicated in Source 4, as he promised the strong leadership the president felt was appropriate for the economic situation. This collapse of democratic government was not only the fault of the economic collapse, but was also the result of the system of proportional representation, which created unstable coalitions. However, this system was to benefit the Nazis as it allowed them to gain a foothold in the Reichstag and to form a legitimate coalition in 1933, which gave them a majority. In the absence of these events, it is doubtful that the Nazi Party would have had such an impact, even with a willingness to resort to violence.

e The answer to part (a) shows sound comprehension, but the comparative points are hinted at rather than developed fully. There is a failure to illustrate the differences effectively with apposite quotations, as candidate A did. This response deserves level 2: 11 marks, although it could easily have earned higher marks with more illustrative analysis.

The answer to part (b) is clearly a causal response, with much accurate and relevant information. Source 5 is used throughout in a supporting role, but Source 4 is largely ignored, apart from a passing reference near the end. This is a serious defect as Source 4 offers much that needs analysis and further exploration. This answer is not driven primarily by the sources provided and thus, despite impressive own knowledge, would be awarded level 2: 18 marks.

Question 3

Source 1: *From an open letter of the German Communist Party addressed to the working voters of the NSDAP and the members of the SA, written in 1931*

In many villages members of the NSDAP, under Communist leadership, have prevented working peasants from having their cows seized or their smallholdings auctioned off.

What did your leaders say about that? They forbade every self-help measure. They admonished you to remain within the law. You're supposed to starve legally.

Social liberation your leaders promised, but they joined together in Harzburg with the leaders of the big trusts and banks, promising them their faithful service. In Harzburg the SA marched in review for the millionaire, Hugenberg, the finance princes and trust lords.

In the economic council of the Brüning government, the big capitalists represented in Harzburg gave their advice along with the Social Democratic Union leaders, on how the wool can be pulled most quickly over the eyes of the working people. And you were expected to help them.

For us there is only one way out — socialism.

Source 2: *From a pamphlet,* National Socialism: A Menace, *published in 1932, written by a conservative critic of the NSDAP*

It is certain that National Socialism does not favour monarchy and is definitely republican in belief. The core of its domestic political programme is the same as that of social democracy on economic, social and tax policy, and largely also in agrarian proposals. Hitler is demanding continuation of the socialist policy that contributed to our economic collapse and harmed the workers as well. His excessive agitation against property and capital, and his unscrupulous provocation of people to militancy, threaten to destroy every possibility of reconstruction by arousing instincts of envy that will not be easily controlled.

Source 3: *From the programme of the German Workers' Party (later to become the NSDAP) drawn up by Hitler and Drexler and made public in February 1920*

12 In view of the enormous sacrifices of life and property demanded of a nation by any war, personal enrichment from war must be regarded as a crime against the nation. We demand therefore the ruthless confiscation of all war profits.

3

13 We demand nationalisation of all businesses which have been formed into corporations (trusts).

14 We demand profit-sharing in large industrial enterprises.

Source 4: *Elections to the Reichstag (% vote)*

Elections	Political parties (% of vote)						
	NSDAP	DNVP	DVP	Centre	DDP	SPD	KPD
May 1924	6.5	19.5	9.5	16.6	5.7	21.6	12.6
December 1924	3.0	20.5	10.1	17.3	6.3	26.0	9.0
May 1928	2.6	14.2	8.7	15.2	4.8	29.8	10.6
September 1930	18.3	7.0	4.9	14.8	3.5	24.5	13.1
July 1932	37.3	5.9	1.2	15.7	1.0	21.6	14.3
November 1932	33.1	8.5	1.8	15.0	1.0	20.4	16.9

Source 5: *From* Germans into Nazis *by Peter Fritzsche, published in 1998*

Although Hitler's appointment to the Chancellorship at the end of January 1933 hinged on the closed-door negotiations of conservatives and out and out monarchists such as Paul von Hindenburg, Alfred Hugenberg and especially Franz von Papen, Hitler would never have figured in their calculus had he not been the leader of Germany's largest party. Much as local élites such as landowners, merchants and clergymen worked with and in due course made National Socialists respectable, Nazi success rested on a broader popular uprising that had challenged and undercut the power of conservative notables throughout the 1920s.

(a) **Study Sources 1, 2 and 3.**
   How far do these three sources support the opinion that the Nazi Party between 1920 and 1933 was a party of the political right?
   (20 marks)
(b) **Study Sources 4 and 5 and use your own knowledge.**
   Did Hitler come to power as a result of secret deals with conservatives or as a result of a broad public support?
   (40 marks)

■ ■ ■

Answer to question 3: candidate A

(a) The sources, which range over 12 years, indicate that the Nazi Party contained aspects of political thought belonging to both the left and the right. Source 2 indicates that the Nazis challenged the traditional views of the right regarding the monarchy, and it accuses them of having socialist views: 'The core of its domestic political programme is the same as that of social democracy on economic, social and tax policy, and largely also in agrarian proposals.' This is supported by the third source, although this is from 10 years before the other two. The demand for nationalisation and profit sharing does not indicate a party of the right, which Source 1 accuses the Nazi leadership of being. The Nazi leaders are accused, by Source 1, of joining with the 'finance princes' and 'big capitalists', which would indicate that they are very much a party of the right. This runs completely contrary to Source 2. These positions might be expected, however, as the two sources express the opinions of the Nazis' political rivals. The Communists in Source 1 clearly wish to damage the Nazis as they are both rivals for the working-class vote, and the author of Source 2 wishes to do the same from a conservative perspective. It is significant that even Source 1 acknowledges the radical militancy of the Nazi rank and file, in this way agreeing with Source 2. None of the sources date from 1933 and it is possible that policies changed. Overall, the three sources do not make a convincing case for the NSDAP being a party of the right in these years.

(b) Source 5 draws attention to key factors in Hitler's coming to power in January 1933. The source makes the point that he was appointed chancellor following 'closed-door negotiations' with key figures among the political élite. The source also argues that these figures were only interested in him because he enjoyed the support that came from 'a broader popular uprising'. This popular support can be illustrated by reference to the election statistics provided in Source 4.

There can be little doubt that Hitler enjoyed broad support by 1932. As Source 5 indicates, he was the leader of Germany's largest party. In the Reichstag elections of July 1932 the NSDAP attracted over 37% of the popular vote, making it the most popular party in the history of the Weimar Republic. Despite the setbacks in November 1932, it was still the most popular of the German parties and, as Source 5 points out, its success had been bought at the expense of the other political groupings of the right, the DVP and the DNVP. Since 1929, the NSDAP had attracted increasing support from various groups. Initially, these had been the young and new voters and the peasantry. As the Communist Party had grown in strength as the slump intensified, more and more of the middle classes had switched to the Nazis as their only possible defenders. Unlike other parties, the Nazis appeared to draw support from different social and religious groups and different geographical regions of Germany. Hitler therefore had a claim to become chancellor in 1932 on the basis of the electoral support he enjoyed. He did not, however, have a majority, and to achieve this he would need to make a deal with one or more of the other parties, i.e. create a coalition, like every other government of Weimar Germany. Hence 'the closed-door negotiations'.

The key figures who brought Hitler to power are mentioned in Source 5. The president, Paul von Hindenburg, was crucial, as without his agreement Hitler could not be chancellor. His opposition to Hitler had kept him from the post in July 1932. Franz von Papen led a splinter group of the Centre Party and Hugenberg was the leader of the DNVP. In January, von Papen played the key role (indicated in Source 5 by the use of the word 'especially'). He had been chancellor in 1932 but was forced from power in November after failing to secure a majority in the Reichstag and losing the support of the influential political general von Schleicher, who replaced him as chancellor. Von Papen sought to return to power and used his influence with Hindenburg to persuade him to accept Hitler, whom he argued could be controlled as chancellor. The deal von Papen brokered involved Hindenburg appointing Hitler as chancellor, but with only two other Nazis in the cabinet and Hugenberg of the DNVP controlling the economy. The theory was that Hitler would deliver the seats in the Reichstag, enabling a return to constitutional government that had been abandoned in 1930. Hitler's appointment would thus be a return to a form of parliamentary democracy.

Hitler therefore came to power both as a result of negotiations with figures on the right, as indicated in Source 5, but also, as Source 5 indicates and Source 4 shows, because he enjoyed more popular support than any other political leader.

e The response to part (a) is excellent and deserves almost full marks (level 3: 19 marks). All three sources are used intelligently (i.e. they are not just accepted at their face value) and a real attempt is made to use the attributions provided to assess their worth as evidence. Source 1 is used effectively, not just to indicate a simple point of view (i.e. the Nazis were a party of the right) but to illustrate the apparent differences between leaders and followers. Quotations are selected and deployed well to make a case.

The response to part (b) is also excellent, being driven by the sources, which are repeatedly used in conjunction with relevant own knowledge. There is a sustained focus throughout on the exact wording of the question. The conclusion is possibly a little too brief. Overall, this response would secure level 4: 38 marks.

■ ■ ■

Answer to question 3: candidate B

(a) Source 1 indicates that the Nazis were a party of the political right because the Nazi leaders had joined with Hugenberg, who was the leader of the DNVP. The DNVP was a monarchist party that hated the Communists and the SPD and wanted a more authoritarian Germany, which its members hoped that Hitler would help them to get. He ultimately did do this in 1933. Source 2 represents a totally different viewpoint and indicates that the Nazis were a party of the political left: 'His excessive agitation against property and capital and his unscrupulous provocation of people to militancy, threaten to destroy every possibility of reconstruction by arousing instincts of envy that will not be easily controlled.' Source 3 seems to agree with Source 2, but it is from 10 years earlier. It seems to indicate that the

Nazis were against profits and for socialism. The title also indicates that they had been called the German Workers' Party originally.

(b) Hitler came to power as a result of many factors. First, he was a charismatic and brilliant politician. He was an outstanding speaker and skilful manipulator of others. He was backed by a politician of genius in Goebbels, who played a major role in presenting the NSDAP to the German people.

The vital ingredient in Nazi success was, however, the slump of 1929–33. By 1932 there were 6 million unemployed, 33% of the workforce. Many who were not registered as unemployed, such as farmers and small shopkeepers, were also in dire poverty. There was a tidal wave of misery and hopelessness, which engulfed the Weimar Republic. Crime rose and there seemed the prospect of a Communist revolution as votes for the Communist Party rose. The Nazis had been a small and insignificant party in 1928, as Source 4 shows, but support for them grew rapidly. They gained the support of large numbers of farmers in the 1930 election and became the second largest party. As the slump intensified, so their support multiplied. Hitler came second to Hindenburg in the presidential election of spring 1932 and in the summer of that year the Nazis became the largest party in the Reichstag by a considerable margin.

Luck also played a key part in the Nazis' triumph. The ban on Hitler speaking, imposed after the Munich Putsch of 1923, was lifted just as the slump began. It seemed that in 1928 he was no real threat to anybody but this, as shown above, was changed by economic circumstances. The vote on the Young Plan in 1929 gave Hitler a chance to become a national politician, backed by wealthy conservatives like Hugenberg, who launched a common campaign with the Nazis against the proposed deal on reparations negotiated by Stresemann. Stresemann was the key figure in most Weimar coalition governments but he died in October 1929, making it more difficult to achieve stability. The chancellor appointed by Hindenburg in March 1930, Brüning, called an unnecessary election in September 1930, which gave the Nazis their chance in the elections of that year. The dismissal of Brüning in 1932 and the appointment of von Papen led to another election, which helped the Nazis. They had enjoyed a remarkable run of good fortune.

The final breakthrough came when von Papen persuaded the president to accept Hitler as chancellor in January 1933. This was another example of luck, because Nazi support was falling, as the November elections showed, and the slump was beginning to lift. Hitler was certainly able but he was also very, very lucky.

> *e* This candidate's answer to part (a) is not as good as that of candidate A. Only the attribution of Source 3 is used, and in a limited way. A comparison is made between Source 1 and Source 2, but in a very straightforward fashion. Source 1 is developed by accurate own knowledge, which is not called for in this question. The use of quotations is ineffective because of the candidate's failure to select precisely (level 2: 10 marks).

3

The answer to part (b) is clearly causal and focuses on the reasons for Hitler coming to power, but it is not driven by the sources; these are barely used, although Source 4 is acknowledged implicitly. This is a classic example of a well-informed candidate throwing away chances of success by ignoring the sources. The response deserves a high level 2: 19 marks.